PERGAMON INSTITUTE OF ENGLISH (OXFORD)

Language Teaching Methodology Series

ENGLISH AT SCHOOL:
THE WOOD AND THE TREES

A manual for teachers of English as a mother tongue

Other titles in the series

BRUMFIT, C J
Problems and principles in English teaching

CARROLL, B J
Testing communicative performance

KELLERMANN, M
The forgotten third skill: reading a foreign language

LEONTIEV, A A
Psychology in the language learning process

NEWMARK, P P
Aspects of translation

ROBINSON, P
English for Special Purposes: the present position

ENGLISH AT SCHOOL: THE WOOD AND THE TREES

A manual for teachers of English as a mother tongue

DERRICK SHARP

Senior Lecturer in Education
University College of Swansea

PERGAMON PRESS
Oxford · New York · Toronto · Sydney · Paris · Frankfurt

UK	Pergamon Press Ltd, Headington Hill Hall, Oxford OX3 0BW, England
USA	Pergamon Press Inc, Maxwell House, Fairview Park, Elmsford, New York 10523, USA
CANADA	Pergamon of Canada, Suite 104, 150 Consumers Road, Willowdale, Ontario M2J IP9, Canada
AUSTRALIA	Pergamon Press (Aust) Pty Ltd, PO Box 544, Potts Point, NSW 2011, Australia
FRANCE	Pergamon Press SARL, 24 rue des Ecoles, 75240 Paris, Cedex 05, France
FEDERAL REPUBLIC OF GERMANY	Pergamon Press GmbH, 6242 Kronberg-Taunus, Pferdstrasse 1, Federal Republic of Germany

SB 11299 £5.95. 3.80

Copyright © 1980 Pergamon Press Ltd.

First edition 1980

British Library Cataloguing in Publication Data

Sharp, Derrick
English at School. – (Pergamon Institute
of English (Oxford). Language teaching methodology
series).
1. English language – Study and teaching
I. Title
420'.7 PE1065 79–40705

ISBN 0-08-024553-6 hardcover
ISBN 0-08-024552-8 flexicover

Text set in 10/12 pt VIP Sabon, printed and bound in Great Britain at The Pitman Press, Bath

For Barbara

Contents

Introduction

The aim in this book is to survey the field of the teaching and learning of English as mother tongue in order to offer practical help to hard-pressed teachers, and to suggest ways of approach for students training for the profession. The emphasis throughout is on fundamental principles which should determine work in the classroom. These include guidelines for English activities and also suggestions which it is hoped will aid the planning of an English programme, for we need a structure which is flexible and which avoids rigid sequencing.

The work is deliberately limited in length so that the reader may take into account the whole survey, but because deeper study is necessary as well there are frequent references and suggestions for further exploration. The writer has had particularly in mind the many teachers described on page 5 '. . . . who tend to feel lost as a consequence of the vast range of theory and practice which has confronted them in recent years. They are conscious of the need to examine their own practice and the theoretical basis of it, but for varied reasons they find it extremely difficult to reach a true understanding in the often limited time available to them. They may be specialists with long experience; they may be non-specialists in the secondary school whose English work is only a part, perhaps very small, of their week; they may be primary school teachers who are aware of the importance of language but who face many competing demands on their time and energy. A very real problem faces such people when they attempt to understand and incorporate the multitude of ideas and suggestions current in the world of English teaching'.

There is no attempt, therefore, to introduce new theoretical arguments but rather to propose a set of logical and practical principles, at a time characterized by a bewildering profusion of often conflicting theories.

The author, drawing on his experience as a teacher, teacher-trainer and director of two Schools Council projects, has sought to supplement his theses with discussions of practical difficulties and references to a wide range of relevant literature, including the Bullock report, *A language for life*. The three basic chapters on language and literature are followed by summaries of salient points as guides to good practice. Finally, the author sums up his concept of the role and function of English mother-tongue teaching.

English is seen as a central part of a liberal education, which ensures the development of the whole person and not just the intellect. Personal, emotional and social development must be part of our concern in a properly balanced way (see pages 117–118, the concluding summary of principles). But these aspects are not explored in the book except as they occur in the discussion of the practical problems of teaching, and comments and suggestions are based on classroom practice and observation.

Some areas are not covered except by incidental reference. They include, for example, the multiracial and multicultural classroom and sex differentiation, especially as it affects the study of literature. These are seen as most important, but they are so complex and work on them is at such a comparatively early stage that they would confuse the immediate issues in this book. More work is clearly needed in order to draw together even more threads, including the search for common ground with the teaching of foreign languages and English as a second or foreign language. The current efforts of the National Congress on Languages in Education and the Language Steering Committee are referred to in the discussion of language study on pages 52–56.

The ideas and conclusions put forward for discussion have been shaped and influenced over many years by colleagues, friends, students and pupils. To try to list them would be foolhardy, but their contribution is acknowledged and appreciated.

1. The present state

Since the end of the second world war, we in Great Britain have seen rapid and extensive changes in all spheres of education, so much so that even the most progressive of us must at times long for some of the stability that characterized the previous system. Before the 1944 Education Act change did take place, of course, but it was in general piecemeal and comparatively slow, because the main efforts were concentrated on the achievement and consolidation of universal literacy in the elementary schools and the full development of secondary and higher education. By 1939 the weaknesses in the system had become evident, especially in the light of developments in society itself. Since then most attention has been focused on alterations in the structure of education but these in turn have raised issues in the fields of content and method, so that the last fifteen years have seen, for the first time on any significant scale, resources devoted to curriculum research and development and an unprecedented amount of individual and group concern and activity in the same area. It is tempting to explore the general picture in more detail, but the purpose of this book is to concentrate on a limited, but nevertheless substantial, part of it—the teaching and learning of English.

The changes in English work in schools have been at least as rapid and far-reaching as developments in other curriculum areas and the controversy has at times been fierce, partly because everyone in the country speaks English and regards himself as qualified to pronounce, partly because one important aspect of English work, the functional or the use of language to communicate with other human beings as a necessary part of living, affects all members of society in many different ways and partly because some features, notably spelling, punctuation and 'correct grammar', can, it seems, be readily assessed and discussed at length in the correspondence columns. Some of the issues, such as the value of formal grammar, have a long history;

others, such as the place of English in integrated studies, are comparatively recent in origin. What are the outward signs of what has been and is happening? Older readers will have an advantage in that they can compare their own experience in one decade with that in another, but all teachers of English can at least draw comparisons between their present knowledge and attitudes and those of their school and college days.

1. There is now as much importance given to learning as to teaching, so that it is almost automatic to write 'the teaching and learning of English', as at the end of the previous paragraph, rather than simply 'the teaching of English'. The emphasis has moved from the teacher on the pedestal, imparting knowledge and training skills, to the cooperative effort of pupil and teacher in the learning process. Frank Whitehead (1966) was amongst the first to draw attention to the change and its implications by entitling his book *The disappearing dais* and examining the effects chapter by chapter.

2. The change in the number and appearance of English textbooks. There is today a wealth, almost an embarrassment of choice, in contrast to the limited range of uniform editions of literary texts and course books, heavily biased towards grammar, which existed before the war. We have seen the movement from course books to thematic books to source books, and, indeed, the move away from textbooks altogether. Technological advance and new attitudes have led to the bold use of colour and excellent reproduction of photographs, as well as to the new 'machinery' of the classroom, in which film, radio, records, slides, tapes, television and even closed-circuit television are becoming as familiar as blackboard and chalk. To all this must be added the availability of kits or packs of materials, which many teachers find most useful in the organization of individual and group work, especially for mixed-ability classes.

3. The growth in the opportunities for in-service training, fostered by, but not initiated solely by, the spreading network of teachers centres. Courses on offer cover the range of English activities and concerns, from linguistics to workshops, from creativity to accu-

racy, from oracy to the organization of an English department, and they are sponsored by too many institutions and organizations to attempt a list here. Conferences and other opportunities for discussion and exploration are also provided by the voluntary associations of teachers of English, not only in Britain, but also in an increasing number of other countries with the same or similar problems and challenges.

4. The rapid expansion in the number of research and development projects which are concerned with various aspects of English in education. It would be invidious to mention some without attempting the task of listing all, but the general work of the Schools Council should be acknowledged. Perhaps it was inevitable that the early, sudden profusion of projects, even within the comparatively limited field of English, should have a bewildering effect on many teachers. A recent emphasis on dissemination of knowledge and materials coming from projects indicates that the lesson has been learnt. The reader is left to supply his own examples and may add local group projects probably unknown to the author.

5. The development of a new concern, initially referred to by several names such as language for learning and the mother-tongue medium of teaching, but crystallized first by the London Association for the Teaching of English and then by the *Bullock report* (Chapter 12, 1975) as *language across the curriculum*. This is dealt with in Chapter 6 (pages 79–87).

This list could be extended, and perhaps will be by the reader. The point has been made. Some changes reflect trends in the larger sphere, as when a teacher's English work is conditioned by his awareness of social injustice and the literature associated with attempts to right wrongs. (*See* John Dixon's (1975) valuable exploration of three models of English—skills, cultural heritage and personal growth—in 'A method of definition', Chapter 1 of *Growth through English*.) Some changes may be considered as peculiarly within his own domain, as when a teacher decides to base all his work on the appreciation and writing of poetry. Yet others may start in this way within the province of the teacher of English and then be found to bear implications extending far beyond the limits of the subject, difficult as the boundaries are to draw; the most obvious example of this in recent years, covered in part by (5) above, has been the way in which those who have worked on the language development of children in order to improve English language learning and teaching procedures have come to realize, with the help of psychologists and sociologists, that this is not a concern properly restricted to the English lesson, but that it conditions all the pupil's learning and indeed his living; moreover, the teacher's own use of language is seen to be equally significant in the total process of interaction.

What are the consequences of the constant challenging of traditional assumptions and the many advocacies of new approaches and different emphases? What is the present state of English teaching in Britain? This is a simple and valid question to ask, but it is impossible to give anything like a simple or precise answer. Change has certainly taken place during the last 30 years and it is probably true to suggest that no teacher of English has remained completely unaffected by the climate, but equally certainly change has occurred unevenly, and it is possible to find in the schools a very wide range of practice, from the rigidly traditional to the extremely progressive, because the individual school and teacher quite rightly retain a considerable degree of freedom of choice. There has in many quarters been a commendable reaction against formal methods and the wholesale use of language exercises, in favour of more creative work and greater freedom for the pupil, but there has also been a clinging to tradition by those who refuse to reject the 'brick-upon-brick' approach to native language acquisition and who maintain in face of the evidence that no-one can use his language unless he knows (consciously) how it works. In between the two extremes there are many teachers of English who have adopted new approaches and materials with caution, and even within this group there is a wide range from those who have combined successfully new and traditional elements to those who, perhaps under pressure, have introduced one new feature which is completely out of keeping with the main part of their work. The variation in practice may be found within the same school, often it is found within the schools of one area. On the other hand, differences may be basically geographic in nature, perhaps as a result of an active inspector or group of teachers in one area, so that while it might be appropriate in one area to discuss the many possible ways of encouraging children to write, in another area it would be just as proper to suggest that pupils might be over-stimulated, with the result that the focus of attention moves from the work in hand to the teacher's ingenuity. Rates of change may also vary according to the level of education, because we can safely say that overall greater progress has been made in primary, particularly infants, schools than in secondary schools, while universities are usually the most conservative in their attitudes to change. The *Bullock report* surveys (1975) indicate, however, that formal methods, especially various forms of language study, are still more widespread at all levels than we sometimes like to think.

It is probably more helpful to view the present state of English teaching from a different angle, by considering how new ideas and more effective methods come to be understood and adopted by teachers and by trying to determine how the process of change can be speeded up and help given to those who are seeking it. Many teachers of English are firm in their conviction that their ways are best, whether they be formal or informal; some of them are open to argument and development, others are not; they include some of the best teachers and some of the worst, but in either case if they feel they need help they know where and how to seek it, because they have deliberately adopted a certain position after due thought.

There is another large group, however, who tend to feel lost as a consequence of the vast range of theory and practice which has confronted them in recent years. They are conscious of the need to examine their own practice and the theoretical basis of it, but for varied reasons they find it extremely difficult to reach a true understanding in the often limited time available to them. They may be specialists with long experience; they may be non-specialists in the secondary school whose English work is only a part, perhaps very small, of their week; they may be primary school teachers who are aware of the importance of language but who face many competing demands on their time and energy. A very real problem faces such people when they attempt to understand and incorporate the multitude of ideas and suggestions current in the world of English teaching. In this sense, the present state is not only confused but also confusing, and one can understand, though not accept, the attitude of those who develop a routine in the classroom and refuse to be affected by change, concentrating instead on outside interests.

Nor do we know how to assess methods and materials properly. Because teaching is both an art and a science, there must always be a subjective element in our judgment of the value of one approach compared with another and our evaluation of the result of X's work in the classroom. Language development and the growth of response to literature are long-term processes which cannot be measured from week to week or month to month, though some try to do this and succeed usually in examining only superficialities or trivia which are readily susceptible to measurement. Examinations in English are a complex and controversial area, reflecting in a very real way the impossibility of answering the relevant question when we are considering the range of classroom practice: Who is right? This is not to deny that some weaknesses and misconceptions can be demonstrated [Harris (1965)], some practices condemned by general agreement and success recognized by talking to pupils and teachers, but it does mean that we often have to proceed by affirmation and persuasion, basing our arguments on our own experience and finding it difficult to convince those who demand proof.

The range of practice in existence and the genuine, deeply-rooted differences of opinion lead, for example, to competing demands for a literature-based as opposed to a language-based syllabus. Debate has raged fiercely, too, over the content of English, embracing some suggestion that there is no clearly-defined content, or at least that knowledge, particularly about literature and/or language, has no value. This point figured in the discussions at the first large-scale international conference devoted to the teaching of English, held in the late summer of 1966 at Dartmouth College in the United States of America, as did other controversial issues which had not previously been properly realized or examined, but which have since seized the attention of many teachers and educationalists. The Dartmouth Seminar and the wider-based International Conference at the University of York in July 1971, illustrate one approach to the central problem, one way of attempting to understand and reconcile divergent opinions and practices. But at the same time the size of the problem is shown, for instance, by a study of the two reports published after the Dartmouth Seminar [Dixon (1967); Muller (1967)], for each is a true reflection of what took place and yet they are very different indeed in selection, emphasis and conclusions drawn, even allowing for the fact that one was written for the professional audience and the other, the American, for the public at large.

Since 1966 there has been in this country an increasing interest in and demand for cohesion or integration in school work in English, a mounting concern about the fragmentation which has followed the entirely healthy rejection of many traditional practices and which has caused the confusion and sense of wandering somewhat aimlessly felt by teachers of English in many schools. The situation has been aggravated by the over-zealous claims of some to have found the cure for all our ills, so that we have been subjected to a series of demands that we should base all our English teaching on this aspect or that skill. Teachers tend instinctively to distrust 'fashions', and there is a real danger that much of true value will not be given a fair trial because of the general climate of feverish change. It is easy to exaggerate the confusion, of course, for certainly it does not affect all teachers of English, but there is sufficient unease about this particular situation to make the demand for cohesion a real and important one, as is witnessed whenever groups meet for discussion.

In the minds of many teachers of English the question of organization, balance, continuity, structure, framework, synthesis or progression is the urgent one at present. Yet words are treacherous and no doubt the reader has already started to interpret the various terms used in the last sentence in the light of his own experience and beliefs, because we all tend to read books to confirm our own views (if not prejudices). Those who adopt an extreme position favouring the 'free flow' approach may have ceased to be readers already, while others are happily continuing, confident that at last we are going to finish with all that nonsense and get back to rigidly structured schemes of work, with the progress to be expected each week clearly defined. It is not as easy as that, of course, though it is easy to suggest that the solution lies between the two extremes. The rest of this book will attempt to express as precisely as possible what is meant by structure and how it may be achieved, but there is no one road to salvation in the teaching and learning of English and the structure may not be seen as such by some. Perhaps the use of the singular is misleading, for what is envisaged is in one sense a maze of structures, designed not to baffle but to assist by opening various avenues.

As usual, it is not difficult to explain the kind of structure or framework which is *not* acceptable, either because it has been tried and found inadequate or because it runs contrary to firmly established and valued professional attitudes and rights. Reference has already been made to language exercises, and these may be placed in the context of the traditional course book, whether or not it contains formal grammar. The course book structure is superficially appealing, for it divides the year into its three terms and each term into its component weeks, then assigning work of various kinds to each section with the aim of building successively on the foundation laid. But the use of language out of context, as in vocabulary exercises demanding the meaning of isolated words, or synonyms and antonyms, is of little or no value, and if we have learnt anything in the last 50 years it is that native language development is a unitary process not best fostered by the collection of bits and pieces of language or information about language.

The negative approach is helpful, but we are left with the essential question: How do we assess the various advances in knowledge and understanding, in methodology, and how can we bring the best of them together in the classroom in schemes of work which provide the desired framework?

The suggestions made in the following chapters are firm yet tentative, because progress is made by a sequence of suggestion, trial, discussion, modification, re-trial, more discussion and modification—or it should be. The thinking, indeed the existence of this book, owes much to the author's participation in such group work with both primary and secondary teachers and students in many areas of England and Wales.

One of the most encouraging features of the 'present state' is the growth of combined exploration, whether officially sponsored or the result of individual initiative, in which each member contributes his wisdom, experience and expertise, for we have to accept that the field of English studies is so vast that no one person, however able and industrious, can master its many facets or fully grasp the other disciplines which are now seen to be essential to a true understanding and effective practice.

The difficulty is expressed by Professor James Britton (1970) in the foreword to *Language and learning*:

> Expertise is dangerous, used in the open, and the choice is between taking risks with it or leaving it alone—which, as I judge it, is no choice at all. After all, if I must confess, I am not a philosopher, a psychologist, a sociologist, a linguist *and* a literary critic; for the sake of the confessional I could have said "*or*", but not for the purpose of my argument.'

There certainly is 'no choice at all', for the central concern of pedagogy should be just that synthesis of knowledge and ideas from all relevant disciplines that is so hard to achieve, and impossible to achieve without taking risks. As Britton states, the relevant disciplines for us include linguistics, psychology, sociology, philosophy and literary criticism—and no doubt some readers have decided that one of us (or both) has put them in the wrong order, another illustration of the size of the problem, for as we shall see there are competing schools of thought as to which should dominate. In spite of substantial advances in recent years, we can still truthfully say that we know comparatively little about areas of vital concern, such as the language development of children or the nature of language and its function in society. It would then be logical, though defeatist, to suggest that until the psychologist or linguist or sociologist, for instance, provides us with the necessary information and hypotheses we cannot be expected to develop properly based methods and materials for the teaching and learning processes. Some do believe that it is wrong to change established ways before we know in detail the validity and results of proposed alterations, but we cannot afford to wait upon the findings of research in so many related fields, badly as these are needed. We must proceed in the light of what is available to us at present, and we must equally be prepared to modify, or if necessary radically change, what we do, because there is very little certainty in an area where 'results' are part of the interaction between human beings.

It is comforting to realize that we do not start from scratch, because teachers are professionals and as individuals possess a large body of acquired wisdom and intuition which enables them to operate effectively in the classroom. When their expertise is pooled and agreed methods arrived at, we are on much firmer ground, even though we need still more information and suggestion from the other experts mentioned. Unfortunately, many discussions of the teaching of English in recent years have been bedevilled by a blinkered approach, by an insane desire to exclude all but the favoured approach, to see no good at all in alternative methods. It is difficult to understand why, for example, a realization of the value of 'creative writing' should lead teachers in a junior school to abandon all other types of English work in order to concentrate on the one chosen aspect. It is even more difficult to understand the choice of 'reading for information' as the sole English activity.

The plea is for synthesis, therefore, the search is for organization, structure, framework, continuity, progression or whatever concept emerges as the most suitable for the model suggested. The key questions are:

1. What activities should we include under the heading of 'English'?
2. What principles should inform English work in the classroom?
3. What should be the unifying feature which makes sense of the whole process?

Unless we seek answers which are clear-cut but not rigid, we shall leave many teachers of English confused as at present and we may even confirm in their beliefs those who reject new ideas on principle and teach as they were taught, without any consideration of whether they were taught well or badly. The unified scheme must also retain the essential freedom of choice of the teacher and the learners to decide what is most suitable for their particular needs and situations.

A final point should be made in this chapter. Although it is argued that structure has to be provided by one basic approach, it is worth repeating and emphasizing that the choice of one as the unifying force does not mean the automatic rejection of all others. To advocate language development is not to deny the vital importance of literature.

2. Balance of activities

The problem

The crucial question here is: How do we plan a year's work in English? On a larger scale, how do we plan progression in English for the four years of the junior-school, or the five years of the secondary-school course?

The traditional answer has been, and still is in many schools, the course book or work-book, which in general contains three sections, one for each term, with ten chapters, one for each week, in each section. The course consists of four books for the junior school or five for the secondary school, though there are several variations on the theme, and in any case schools have not always used all the books in a series. For some reason, the fifth book of any secondary course has been less popular than the earlier books. Each chapter in such a course book contains a mixture of exercises, some substantial, some slight, embracing such aspects as composition, comprehension, vocabulary, spelling, punctuation and correction of sentences. Not all aspects appear in each chapter, for the mixture varies according to the age and abilities of the pupils for whom the work is designed and according to the comparative importance of the aspects at the particular level of development. Thus summary or *précis* work will appear in books for fourth and fifth year secondary pupils but not at all in books for junior schools.

The course book has many advantages. For the teacher, it provides a scheme, it gives the appearance of logical progress, it provides work which can easily be set for homework and which can readily be tested, and it can mean little or no preparation of lessons. For the pupil, it has a neat structure, it includes interesting material (in the best cases) and it gives a sense of achievement as each stage is 'ticked off'. Sometimes the sense of achievement is an illusion, for the exercises are very easy indeed. But these advantages, and others the reader may claim to be of equal importance, are not to be despised, because teachers are often hard pressed and lack the time or ability to devise their own schemes, and most of us need to see shape or structure in whatever we are doing. The objections to the kind of structure provided by a course book are even more telling, however.

Linguistic development in the mother tongue is not like building a wall, adding brick to brick until the whole is complete and regular. Nor is it even and sequential, as the wall image, the basis of the course book approach, would imply. Furthermore, the ability to complete correctly a language exercise such as correction of sentences does not necessarily lead to an equivalent improvement in general language usage, either in speech or in writing, as we are only too well aware. Purposeful language development is achieved by using and responding to language in context, and the course-book exercise rarely provides more than a minimal context, if that. These matters will be considered more fully in Chapters 3 and 4. The worst course books, and there are many bad ones in existence and use, are dull and trivial, while the better ones go out of date but are retained because they represent a considerable financial investment, especially nowadays.

During the last 30 years the situation has been complicated by a series of 'fashions' in English teaching, as mentioned in Chapter 1, including creative writing, themes, reading for information, integrated schemes, projects and spontaneous drama. Each of these has a great deal to offer, but none is *the* road to salvation or the complete solution to our problem. Oral work, a sadly neglected and imperfectly understood aspect, is another example of a different kind.

The impact of these many claims and counter-claims has naturally varied according to the teacher's training, experience and general attitude, but for many it has meant confusion and for a few despair. At the two extremes we find those who attempt desperately to keep up with the changing fashions and those who react violently against any change and revert to excessively formal approaches. Inevitably there is a considerable amount of misunderstanding, especially in the area of language work. A good example of what can happen is the varied interpretations of what 'creative writing' means. We can find some teachers who state that creative writing necessarily means that spelling is not to be corrected, some who proudly claim that their pupils are 'creating like mad' (unconscious of the ambiguity) and are disconcerted when asked what is being created, some who have been led to see creative writing as a panacea and some who regard a child's oral or written composition as a work of literature, to be worshipped but not critically examined. These aspects, too, will be explored in Chapters 3 and 4.

The confusion is at times increased by the working of the puritan conscience, because some of the activities recommended, and given official approval by the Newsom (1963) and Bullock (1975) reports, are enjoyable for all involved. Should they appear on an English syllabus? Is a discussion lesson work? What have we got to show the HMI? Are not audio-visual aids merely entertainment? Much as we should like to dismiss these attitudes as irrelevant and belonging to the past, they are still strong in some areas. Within the last ten years an Education Committee has solemnly debated the question: 'Is a teacher earning his money by playing records?'

Perhaps the worst confusion has been caused by the advice to abolish planned progression, schemes, structure, syllabus or framework because mother-tongue development cannot be regimented in this way. The extreme position suggests that the teacher should not interfere with the natural language development of the child, that the most he should do is provide a stimulating learning environment. This comes dangerously close to opting out (though like most other attitudes it has an element of value) and in any case it does nothing to meet the needs of those who seek structure, who are not happy unless they can see where they are going, or who are not able or willing to plan their own courses.

So far this book has been at best diagnostic, at worst negative. From this point it will be positive.

The solution

About the only thing we can say with conviction is that there is no one simple solution. But we can open avenues and suggest alternatives which at least go some way towards a solution, and it is helpful to consider a three-fold division of the total field of English teaching and learning:

1. Balance of activities.
2. Methods and approaches.
3. Material or content.

These are separate only for purposes of analysis and discussion, a point worth stressing because we sometimes seem to regard the different aspects of English work as distinct 'subjects', in some schools showing them on the timetable as such. While considering activities, methods and material to some extent separately, then, we must always bear in mind that our ultimate concern is the unity of classroom English, of language development in all spheres of learning and school activity.

There is no adequate way of planning English progress in the short term, in contrast to what can be done in a linear subject such as Mathematics. We can produce an itemized syllabus defining each month's or term's work, but the essential areas of language development are still left vague, or expressed in terms of content rather than of progress. Even if we could be more precise in the crucial areas, the result would be of more use for individual and small group work than for planning a class syllabus, for language development is a highly individual affair, as we all realize. Because development in writing continuous prose, for example, is not even, either for the individual pupil or for the group, the step by step approach to planning, rigid sequencing, is not appropriate, though there are emphases and techniques best suited to different stages from the reception class to the sixth form, of course.

Thus a necessary emphasis on talk in the first stages of schooling is followed by the natural stress on reading and then on writing as these skills are gradually acquired. Similarly, spontaneous or free drama normally precedes scripted drama, while critical appreciation of prose style is usually matter for the sixth form. These are simple examples, but the important point is that these and other aspects and features are not in watertight compartments, they occur side by side and each gains emphasis at one point only to lose it at another and perhaps regain it at yet another. To say that narrative poetry is particularly suitable for eleven and twelve year olds is not to suggest the exclusion of lyric poetry but rather that narrative poetry should form a substantial part of poetry work at those ages. To say, as has just been said, that critical appreciation of prose style is usually matter for the sixth form means that for the majority of our able pupils that is the best stage to introduce it, but it does not mean that some few exceptional boys and girls, as individuals or small groups, may not start it earlier.

Sequencing is also inappropriate because language acquisition does not work like that. We may praise a six year old for the proper and effective use of the conditional or relative clauses, whereas in a sequential scheme he might not be handling either at that age. It would be ideal if we could take into account the many complexities and still grade reading material according to language difficulty, but we cannot, except at the simplest levels. In practice we are constantly grading reading matter in a rough and ready way, subjectively in the light of experience and, aided by trial and error, with a fair amount of success, though even then we often pay more attention to subject matter than to language difficulty and we have prejudices and set notions. In particular, we too readily decide that a poem or book is too difficult for a certain age group. The vast area of linguistic analysis for educational purposes has as yet barely been touched, in spite of the advances made by modern linguistics in recent years.

Planning a course

The child's language development is the basis of our English work in schools. Progression in language, in ways to be made clear in Chapters 3 and 4, must provide the framework for our planning. This means that we start with the traditional areas of language activity as shown on Diagram 1, the essential interaction between the areas being indicated by the arrows (see overleaf).

Diagram 1

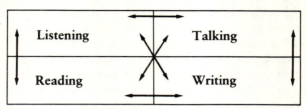

Next we must consider varieties of each of the four: for example, listening to detailed instructions or a serious lecture or a political speech or a cross-talk comedy act; talking argumentatively or persuasively or gossiping; reading a newspaper or a manual or a light novel or a poem; writing a personal account or a business letter or a factual report or a poem. The list in each area is a long one, but not all types of activity are appropriate at all stages in school. For school purposes we may prefer to break down each area differently and consider, for instance, some of the ways in which writing may be divided:

(a) Personal/impersonal. This is a simple division into two categories in order to distinguish between writing in which the writer draws on his own experience, both first-hand and from books and other people, and is *personally* involved, and writing in which his main concern is to communicate facts and information, or to report objectively. The distinction is over-simplified, but it is helpful to realize that personal writing, especially but not only for younger pupils, is a crucial factor in language development.

(b) Narrative/description/explanation/instruction/persuasion/argument.

(c) Registers.[1] Examples known to pupils include the registers of teachers, doctors, sports commentators, fashion writers and scientists.

(d) Transactional/expressive/poetic.[2]

These represent the first, crude stage of thinking for a teacher who is planning a year's writing assignments for a particular class.

If we accept that our aim is to develop the pupil's language ability, his use of and response to language, in each of the four main areas of

Diagram 1, we can place them on a diagram of different shape, for reasons which will become clear later but which include the absence of any order of importance or priority. The undue reverence for reading and writing as the worthwhile activities is still strong in our schools, for understandable historical reasons, and it explains to some extent the slowness and reluctance of the movement towards a proper balance of language activities.

Diagram 2

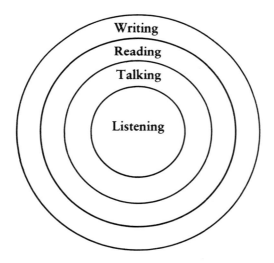

Listening is placed in a central position because it is an essential part of all that we do and yet it comparatively rarely needs specific attention or breaking down into types in the way necessary for other aspects. One primary headmaster known to the writer, however, regards it as so important in language development that he places considerable emphasis on it throughout the first two years in his school and claims that later work in the junior section has benefited greatly. Certainly, attention to listening must figure largely in oral work, though usually in a general way and only occasionally as the focus.

To proceed further with our planning we must take as an example a particular age group. In this case the fourth year in the junior school (age ten-eleven) is chosen because it provides a fairly simple example and because it will not differ radically from the third junior year or the first two secondary years. We then decide which activities of a general type should appear in each of the 'tracks' labelled *Writing*, *Reading* and *Talking* and in what proportions, so that we can sub-divide each track accordingly. Diagram 3 represents one way of doing this, but it is by no means the only way.

Diagram 3: Age ten—eleven

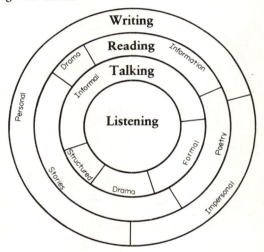

The next stage is to further divide each section of each track, again according to what each teacher, group of teachers or English department considers appropriate. If we continue with the example of *Writing*, we have to decide which types of writing listed under (b) on page 18 should be covered under our two main headings of personal and impersonal, having already determined that by far the greater proportion of writing at this age should be personal, as shown on Diagram 3. We might decide that argument is not suitable at this age, that the personal writing should be almost entirely narrative and description with some persuasion, and that explanation, description and instruction should be evenly spread over the impersonal writing. Alternatively, we might wish to make poetry writing a substantial part of the personal section and the recording of information the whole or most of the impersonal section. If we take another example of a different kind, we can choose from several ways of dividing the poetry-reading section: we can decide that we wish to cover one, two or three types of poetry; we can make a list of the most suitable poems for this age; or we can use a favourite anthology, accepting its arrangement and balance. What matters is that these decisions in all the various sections of the three tracks should be taken in the school, and that they should be reached by consultation among all the teachers involved, even though the ultimate responsibility may rest with one person. The considerations which govern these decisions for the various groups will be explored in later chapters. The emphasis here is on the framework within which planning can take place in such a way as to produce a balanced programme.

The process of sub-dividing each track section is best done separately, in 'boxes', because if all the sub-sub-divisions are written on the diagram it becomes confusingly cluttered, unless one is using a very large diagram indeed.

The structure for the year's work in English is then obtained by a systematic selection from the balance of activities shown on the diagram. If we assume that there are nine full working months in a school year, we can draw radial lines at equal (40°) intervals, as on Diagram 4, and each line gives us the balance of language activities for one month's work.

If the original proportions are right, in the sense that they represent the considered opinion of the teacher or teachers that this is the proper balance for the age group and ability level, the proportions for the year will also be right in the same sense. Care should be taken, however, to make sure that, for example, the drama section of the reading track does not coincide with the drama section of the talking track, because although the activities in drama as part of reading and drama as part of talk are different in many important ways, the similarities between them suggest they are best done at different times in the English programme. Opinions may differ about this, as about many other aspects, of course.

Diagram 4: Age ten—eleven

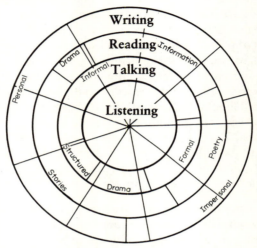

It is not necessary, or even desirable, to take the sequence of monthly schemes in the strict order of rotation of the radial lines. If poetry reading appears as part of the course for only two of the working months, as it does in Diagram 4, the teacher may well decide to take these at different times of the year. Some will object that this is not enough poetry for the year, though it represents more than is covered in the fourth year of many junior schools; they may increase the poetry section of the reading track, of course. Others will state that they prefer to study poems briefly and frequently; they may adjust the diagram by breaking the poetry section into smaller units and placing these so that they appear on more monthly lines, although there is much to be said for blocks of work to achieve continuity in an aspect of English, as opposed to the traditional secondary pattern of one lesson a week on each of five aspects. Adjustment, of which these are examples, is added to earlier decisions about the breakdown of tracks into sub-divisions and sub-sub-divisions to preserve the teacher's freedom of choice and to ensure that, while retaining a desirable balance, pattern, structure or framework, the scheme may be tailored to suit a wide variety of school and classroom circumstances.

Although it will be argued later that some ways are better than others, there are many acceptable ways of dividing and adjusting the diagram tracks. There is no one solution to the problem of organizing English work.

Appropriate materials and schemes of work for the various activities can then be considered separately. It is also possible to start with a body of materials and apply the language activities structure to it, thus catering for those who prefer to begin planning by, for instance, drawing up a list of literary texts.

Language development, practice, training and guidance in the use of and response to a range of language, can be fostered in a balanced series of carefully devised activities and situations or contexts. If properly implemented, the scheme ensures that oral work is not neglected, as it so often still is in our classrooms. Short-term work on points of usage (whether treated grammatically or not), spelling and punctuation can be introduced when the need arises in the flow of spoken and written language which should be the staple of our work. In this way language exercises become occasional and incidental, and not the framework; the tail does not wag the dog. The scheme is flexible, because the choice of track divisions, sequence of monthly lines and materials is an open one, and it is, moreover, adjustable, for if it becomes clear that the proportions or sequence are wrong for a particular class, adjustments may be made during the course of the year.

In short, the scheme is systematic but not rigid.

Notes

1 'The name given to a variety of a language distinguished according to its use is *register*.' (Halliday, McIntosh and Strevens (1964), page 87)

2 These are the function categories defined in *The development of writing abilities (eleven-eighteen)* Britton *et al* (1975):

Transactional 'This is the language to get things done: to inform people, ... to advise or persuade or instruct people' (page 88).

Expressive 'Expressive language is language close to the self.' Often it is 'not made explicit' and is 'relatively unstructured' (page 90). (This is a more perceptive and refined version of the *personal* category in (a) on page 18 above.)

Poetic 'Poetic writing uses language as an art medium'. It is a 'verbal construct', in which the words are selected to make an arrangement, a formal pattern' (page 90). (It is normally a later development in schools.)

Any attempt to define briefly, or to explain the expressive as a matrix for the development of other forms of writing, is bound to be misleading. You should consult *The development of writing abilities (eleven-eighteen)* especially Chapters 5 and 6 (pages 74–105).

3. Language I

'The design of the report is intended to reflect the organic relationship between the various aspects of English, and to emphasize the need for continuity in their development throughout school life.'

This opening sentence on page xxxv of the *Bullock report* draws attention to the unity of English and it is quoted here because the chapter heading above refers to one aspect only, albeit a complex and far-reaching one. It is simply not possible to discuss the principles which should inform English teaching and learning without breaking the subject down in some way, without running the risk of seeming to give undue prominence to one aspect, or even to one detail, while at the same time in the minds of some readers ignoring a vital area.

At this stage it is necessary to affirm again that classroom English is a unitary process. The desirable balance described in Chapter 2 will never be achieved if this fact is overlooked, because progress depends on a flow of language and not on a succession of language items dealt with separately. The itemization which follows in this book is solely to establish the principles which will be used to determine the ways in which the tracks of Chapter 2 should be divided for different ages and ability levels.

The aim, then, is to survey in the small compass of this chapter and the following two the whole field of English language and literature in the classroom in order to establish those principles which should inform all our work. The treatment of each part will inevitably be brief, but this is seen as an advantage. One of our troubles in recent years has been a tendency to concentrate on the trees to the exclusion of the wood; here we are concerned with planning the wood by the careful selection and placing of the trees, and for this purpose a synoptic view is necessary. Equally we must appreciate that this approach will doubtless lead to omissions and misunderstandings, which can be rectified only by further reading, discussion and classroom trial.

The principles arrived at will be summarized at the end of each topic, so that they may readily be used with the diagrams already given. Certain assumptions are made, the most important of which are:

1. The principles remain the same for all ability levels, though the pace and the nature of classroom materials will vary according to ability.

2. The emphases will change according to the age of the pupils. This is easily appreciated in the early years of the primary school, when learning to read and write loom large; it is not so easy to accept and control in the secondary school, when the balance between personal and impersonal writing or the introduction of abstract argument is involved.

The basic principle throughout is that the language development of the child is the criterion. This covers the pupil's use of and response to a wide range of the English language, including its use in literature, as explained in Chapter 5. But this principle is less helpful than it might appear to be, for we have comparatively little firm research evidence about language development, especially in the secondary stage. Nevertheless, in the light of our experience and our firm convictions we must make syllabus decisions in accordance with our view of the contribution to language development made by the activities under consideration.

We must also draw together the threads from many different approaches in our attempt to achieve the best amalgam of language activities in a structured scheme. Although many writers give the impression, at least, that their chosen way is the road to salvation, as opposed to the road to damnation recommended by those who do not agree with them, it is rare to discover in practice that alternative approaches are entirely mutually exclusive. There are clearly important areas where mutual exclusion does operate, and we must not pretend that we can please everybody by taking something from all rival factions. For example, when we are planning a course of children's writing we have to choose between 'accuracy first, 'flow later' and 'flow first, gradually developing accuracy' as basic principles (and later we shall choose the second alternative). But more usually, and again for instance, our preference for narrative poetry with eleven-year-olds does not mean that we must avoid lyric poetry with them, nor should our belief in educational drama exclude a study of scripted drama and theatre at the appropriate stage in the secondary school. It is, of course, a matter of emphasis once the either/or decisions have been made.

To some extent, the exploration of questions of emphasis is what the *Bullock report* is most concerned with, and its 609 pages and 333 conclusions and recommendations give some measure of the size and difficulty of the present task. Just as forcefully they underline the need for this task, because the *Bullock report* requires interpretation in classroom terms and selective comment if its spirit is to survive, as it should, in any planned English course. It seems appropriate at this stage in a work started in 1976 to draw from the report some main points which contribute to the working framework of principles we are seeking.

Although it appears in Part 2 of the report 'Language in the early years', Chapter 4 does in fact by extension and development provide such a framework of principles for 'Language and learning' applicable to all that we do in this area throughout a pupil's years in school. This is not to say that it answers all our questions or solves all our problems, for much of the necessary work, especially in the fields of linguistics and child development, remains to be done. But it does provide the essential basis for professional discussion in the preparation of curriculum and syllabus.

The chapter starts by stressing the role of language 'in *generating* knowledge and *producing new forms* of behaviour', which distin- guishes man from other creatures. With this emphasis on man as a 'symbol-using animal', it examines briefly the way in which language is used to represent the world to ourselves, recognizing that there are also other ways in which we do this. Our major concern is language, however, which is one important means by which we relate present experience to previous experience, building up our 'inner representation' of the world by a process of classification, trial and error, and consolidation. Having skirted the difficult area of the relationship between language and thought, the chapter moves swiftly to a consideration of language used to handle new experiences, not in the simple sense of an extension from past through present to future, but in terms of hypothesis, 'what might be'. The importance of formulation in language as a basis for experiment, modification and further experiment is thus established, with all that this implies for the learning process. There is no space here to cover the chapter in detail, though the reader is urged to consult it for himself, nor to develop the ideas which are so concisely stated in order to reach the classroom implications given in 4.10:

> '(i)   all genuine learning involves discovery, and it is as ridiculous to suppose that teaching begins and ends with 'instruction' as it is to suppose that 'learning by discovery' means leaving children to their own resources;
> (ii) language has a heuristic function; that is to say a child can learn by talking and writing as certainly as he can by listening and reading;
> (iii) to exploit the process of discovery through language in all its uses is the surest means of enabling a child to master his mother tongue.'
>   (Bullock (1975), page 50)

In the first of the Committee's inferences there is a welcome dismissal of the 'black or white' approach, a refusal to accept the two extremes as the only alternatives. In the second there is an implicit call for balance in language activities, as advocated in Chapter 2 of this book, while the third inference recommends a wide range of language usage, a fundamental point covered later.

These ideas are developed in Chapter 5 of the *Bullock report*, which first examines the kind of language usage which the very young, pre-school child needs to develop:

> 'A child is at a disadvantage in lacking the means to explain, describe, inquire, hypothesize, analyse, compare, and deduce if language is seldom or never used for these purposes in his house. This is the kind of language that is of particular importance to the forming of higher order concepts; in short, to learning in the school situation.' (*ibid*, page 54)

On the same page we find stress placed on the need for all children to be 'helped to acquire as wide a range as possible of the uses of language' before entry to school and in the early days of the nursery and infant schools. And we can add that this attention to using and responding to a wide range of language should continue throughout the primary and secondary schools.

The teacher's task is to provide the learning environment, to plan a series of varied experiences, including the very important development of relationships. Initially these will be based on the child's day-to-day experience of living as a member of a community, and this basis should be maintained throughout his school life, although increasingly there is a need and a duty to widen his horizons in many different ways. Time and again the *Bullock report* determines principles for language work with young children which are those very principles which should inform all mother-tongue activities in all schools. In this respect the Committee's Chapters 4 and 5 are seminal.

We find on page 67 that most important sentence:

'We advocate, in short, planned intervention in the child's language development.'

This is a clear statement in principle of the teacher's function. This is what this book is all about. It is true that if a child lives in a human society his language will develop whether he is taught or not. But we are not concerned with this 'natural' development except as it is inevitably part of a total process. Our function as teachers is to stimulate, guide, encourage and plan the child's language development so that in our complex, sophisticated society he may achieve the best command of language of which he is capable. Gradually, but only gradually, we are learning about language and language development in ways which help us to fulfil this function with increasing effectiveness. We certainly realize that 'planning' in this context does not mean the imposition of clear-cut, sequential stages, but rather planning as it is used with reference to anything organic, such as a garden. We may aim at a desired result, but we can never impose a particular pattern, nor can we ever achieve a specific outcome in precise detail. 'Planned intervention' as interpreted throughout the present work is our keynote.

In the same paragraph (5.30) we find an emphasis on keeping records of development, the important concomitant of the kind of structured planning we are examining. There is also a list of the uses of language desirable for the young child's experience. As these are equally applicable to later stages of development, with the addition of persuasion, giving instructions and abstract argument, for example, it is worth reproducing the list here:

'Reporting on present and recalled experiences.
Collaborating towards agreed ends.
Projecting into the future; anticipating and predicting.
Projecting and comparing possible alternatives.
Perceiving causal and dependent relationships.
Giving explanations of how and why things happen.
Expressing and recognizing tentativeness.
Dealing with problems in the imagination and seeing possible solutions.
Creating experiences through the use of imagination.
Justifying behaviour.
Reflecting on feelings, their own and other people's.'

(*ibid*, page 67)

Such a list is of great value to teachers, for they can use it as a prototype, as a basis for discussion in formulating their own school or departmental list of language functions to be covered by their pupils within a specified time, which may be as short as a year or as long as the four years of the junior school or the first five years of the secondary school. Once agreed, the list can be used in three most helpful ways:

(a) in planning the pupil's language experiences;
(b) in reviewing what has been covered to date and then adjusting the programme accordingly; and
(c) in keeping the records mentioned above.

In addition it must be realized, as Chapter 5 makes clear, that there is an important place for unstructured language work in the primary school. Children need to talk to adults as well as to each other, and we must organize the learning environment to allow as much free interaction of this kind as possible.

Other important and relevant topics raised in the report and covered more fully in later sections of this book include the following.

The need to accept a child's accent. (10.5)
The crucial role of awareness and flexibility in language development, so
that pupils may make their own, informed decisions. (10.5)
The notion of *appropriate* language, as opposed to that of *correctness*.
(10.6)
The exploratory use of language, especially talk. (10.11)
The need to develop listening ability as part of ongoing classroom work
rather than in isolation, though it may demand deliberate strategies.
(10.19–10.21)
The central importance of continuity and development, difficult to define
even in pupils' writing but equally needed in talk and listening. (10.24)
Language study is justified if it contributes to language development and
satisfies certain other criteria. (11.1)
The importance of context in all language work. (11.14—made here with
reference to spelling.)
The inclusion of explicit instruction in context to cover certain features of
language—'the need should create the opportunity'. (11.21)
The desirability of appropriate language objectives and the difficulty of
defining them precisely in the present state of knowledge. (11.22, 11.23)

It is tempting to continue in this way, abstracting important strands
from the report, but space forbids and in any case there is no substitute
for study of the original and discussion of how it should be interpreted
and implemented. Some recommendations, such as the establishment
of language centres and the appointment of language consultants, call
for extra money and are unlikely to result in action in the near future,
but others, such as an agreed language policy for a school or an area,
can be achieved at little or no cost. Perhaps it would be appropriate to
leave this concentration on the *Bullock report* by drawing attention to
the first sentence of 11.25:

> 'What we are suggesting, then, is that children should learn about language
> by experiencing it and experimenting with its use.'

and by repeating the phrase which epitomizes the teacher's function:
'planned intervention'.

Certain guidelines emerge from all that we have considered so far. We
should be concerned in all our classroom work with real language (as
explained below) in context. It is comparatively easy to appreciate the
need for context, because we understand more and more about the
ways in which words carry very different meanings or significance in

different situations or when used for differing purposes. Indeed, there is general agreement that one of the teacher's functions is to make older pupils critically aware of this fact by special study of advertising and propaganda, for instance. Consequently an emphasis on words out of context, as in learning lists of words with their synonyms and antonyms, or in defining words in isolation, has largely disappeared from our classrooms. More attention is rightly paid to the flow of language in both speech and writing, although even so the Bullock survey showed that a great deal of lesson time is still spent on language-study exercises in both primary and secondary schools. These exercises are of doubtful value unless they are used to solve specific problems raised in the pupil's own use of or response to the flow of language which must be the staple diet. When they are so used, it should be remembered that the minimum context for practical purposes is one, meaningful sentence (in contrast to the type of sentence so often produced in response to, 'Use these words in separate sentences to show their meanings'—'He is authoritarian.').

The question of 'real' language causes much more trouble. In the minds of many teachers there is a concept of 'correct English', surrounded and supported by rules about split infinitives or starting sentences with conjunctions and ending them with prepositions. Even if they are not too sure of their own grasp of this correct English, they are convinced of its existence and are sure that the right book or person will answer all questions about it. This they use as a yardstick against which they measure their pupils' use of language, in most cases written language because for these teachers the spoken language is a baser form, not usually 'correct' except in very formal situations. As a consequence, they tend to ignore or reduce in importance the oral work which is crucial in language development. The belief in 'one correct English', or the need to create it, is understandable, because life in the classroom is so much easier and more certain if the teacher knows that all answers to language questions are right or wrong.

But real language is not like that. The varieties of English are infinite and our language classroom must accept this fact and live with it. Again, we can more readily accept the differences in writing than in speech, for we are used to varying styles and authors' purposes, while the folk-myths about the spoken language are legion. Some of these problem areas are explored more fully later; at the moment we are concerned more with abstracting general principles. The existence of varieties of English means that in the classroom we should make varying demands on the use of and response to language by our pupils so that they gradually appreciate the idea of English *appropriate* to the circumstances, the nature of the occasion and the people involved—the total context. This appreciation of the concept of *appropriate* English need not be conscious, and indeed in the early years of the primary school it should not be, while some would maintain that it should remain implicit in the pupils' language activities until well into the secondary school.

Naturally, our varying demands on the pupils' language must be selective, for it has already been made clear that some language uses are more sophisticated than others. Our demands on both use and response must be in accord with the situation, the age and the stage of language development of the pupil or group of pupils. Often we learn what is appropriate by trial and error, and by experience, because we need more linguistic knowledge (of the English language and of language development) than is at present available. And many teachers do not know and apply that which is available. The problem of selecting what variety is manageable by primary school children can be severe, but in some situations additional factors complicate an already complex area, especially when learners of English as a second language are involved. They may be in circumstances in which English is heard or seen only in the classroom, or they may encounter considerable community use of English, as do Welsh first language children in Wales and immigrant children in England. In the first case, one variety of English may well be chosen as the target language in the early stages, whereas in the second some range of varieties, however restricted, is essential. Such situations need specific attention in detail at certain stages, but the general principles to be adopted should remain the same. It follows, therefore, that knowledge and experience gained in one type of learning situation are of value in others.

One other aspect of varieties of English needs clarification. The accusation is often levelled that by admitting to our language activities a whole range of 'Englishes', registers, dialects and accents, and by accepting that each is appropriate in its proper context, we are lowering or even abandoning standards. This arises from a misunderstanding of what is being said, and a reluctance to forsake the one, correct, formal English concept. Criteria or standards are just as relevant to the use of appropriateness as the main measure itself. Whenever academic English, for example, is appropriate it must be as precise and formal as ever, while all varieties of English used and encountered must be precise and effective in their own different ways. A major problem for the teacher is that there are so many more standards to take into account in this more realistic approach, and there is no sure way of measuring appropriateness. This is healthy in that it leads to frequent and critical discussion of language varieties as the pupil grows older in the secondary school. For the majority this approach presents no major difficulties, but for those pupils who find it difficult or impossible to respond to or achieve in their own usage the level of formal English corresponding to their age or stage of development the path is sometimes not so smooth. Many of us still tend to measure mother-tongue development on the academic scale, which demands a mastery of formal English, and to regard as failures those who cannot achieve it, whose reading and writing are at best uncertain. We must learn to recognize in the classroom what we accept in a somewhat different form in literature, that effective use of language is not restricted to one style, level or variety.

If standards are lowered, then, it is not the inevitable consequence of varying language demands of the kind covered above. Often standards do suffer because the teacher mistakenly thinks that spelling does not matter at all, perhaps, or that children should not be 'stretched' in their language activities. We must plan our learning environments, our sequences of varying language demands to provide a firm base within the pupil's competence and at the same time give him a sufficient challenge to ensure progress, and advice when he needs it.

Before leaving the topic of real language, we should look more closely at some interpretations of the word 'real' itself, again in order to clarify the ideas which determine our classroom practice. If we urge some classes to use the real language of the street, the factory floor or the home, we shall find that their speech or writing is well larded with 'bad' language. (That adjective provides a stimulating topic for older secondary pupils, incidentally. 'Why is swearing *bad* language?', 'What other kinds of bad language are there?' These two questions can lead in many directions.) Some few teachers are quite happy with a preponderance of bad language in their classrooms. Most are not, and so we realize, and we make the point with our pupils, that like Wordsworth we are properly concerned with a selection from real language. Once more with older pupils this can lead to an appreciation at the conscious level of the social conventions of language ('linguistic table manners'), some of which have been grasped and acted upon without explicit formulation since pre-school days.

The search for realism in the classroom often causes dissatisfaction with the teacher as the sole audience, with the artificiality and lack of 'real' motivation in much of the language work, especially in writing but also in speech. It is clearly helpful if pupils can write real letters to a friend who is really ill in hospital, or real letters thanking the cinema manager who put on a special show for the school, or real letters of complaint about the local bus service, and so on. (Though one sometimes wonders about the effect of the arrival of 30 or so usually very similar letters!) Such occurrences are rare, however, and once they have to be created, or the teacher says, 'I shall send only the best letter', we are back to the 'real' classroom. Similarly it has become increasingly popular to send pupils out into the neighbourhood to conduct real interviews with senior citizens and housewives, presumably because they are available and have time to spare! For the pupils this is a most valuable oral exercise, but it can easily be overdone, so that senior citizens and housewives run screaming at the sight of a teenager with clip-board or cassette recorder. Let us be quite clear that whenever the opportunity arises for genuine, first-hand language work of these kinds we seize it gladly, but that most of the time we need to *create* situations in the classroom and however good our simulation is there is at least some degree of artificiality. This does not matter. What does matter is that the real language in the classroom should be placed in context and that it should be used or commented on for specific purposes by specified people (often the pupils themselves, of course).

Language should not be abstracted from experience and treated as bits and pieces in a vacuum.

Earlier in this chapter we looked at a list of language uses recommended by the Bullock Committee for young children, and suggested the usefulness of such lists for all teachers. In the light of the later discussion of real language in context, involving as it does varieties of English, it is worth returning to the topic for two reasons. The first is to refer the reader to the brief but helpful consideration of different approaches to the classification of language functions by Andrew Wilkinson in *Language and education* (Wilkinson (1975), pages 54–57). He states:

> 'Various people have made lists of language functions, but there is as yet no agreement as to how many significant uses we should take account of. It depends partly on the purpose for which we want to use the list, partly on how detailed we want to be.'

He then examines three examples of models of language:
1. The seven functions of M A K Halliday—instrumental, regulatory, interactional, heuristic, personal, imaginative, and representational.
2. The function categories for writing of J N Britton already mentioned on pages 23–24.
3. The division of language uses by Joan Tough into two—the 'relational' and the 'ideational'.

As already argued, the examination of other people's lists is the first step towards the only valid list for classroom purposes, that drawn up by a teacher and his colleagues, with full knowledge of the particular pupils and circumstances.

The second reason is to consider the planning of varying language demands from a slightly different point of view. Quite rightly we should ensure that the learning situations we devise cover differing functions of language as drawn up in the lists mentioned. In the primary school this approach, carefully worked out and conscientiously followed, is probably sufficient for language development at that stage. It is also adequate for the steady increase in subtlety which should follow, but with secondary pupils we need also to consider the demands of the situation, including the people involved. This is often a more direct guide to planning classroom language activities than is an attempt to refine by sub-division our list of language functions to be covered. It is especially helpful when we are using role-playing for the development and appreciation of varying language uses and responses. If we are concerned with the function of persuasion, for example, we may plan a series of situations which start with the familiar and work out from there, with the pupil 'acting' as himself and as the others involved in the episodes in the sequence. Thus he might move from being himself persuading his father to increase his pocket money, or his headmaster that he does not deserve punishment, or his girl-friend to go to a football match with him, to taking the part, in turn, of his father, his headmaster and his girl-friend. The example is deliberately restricted to the simpler kind of situation in order to establish the principle. Notice that it would be natural to carry out this work orally, but that even in these simple situations circumstances might arise in which it would be necessary or tactically desirable to conduct negotiations in writing.

Obviously teachers are using this approach in hundreds of classrooms across the school age-range every day, but in many cases the choice of situation, of language demands in role-playing is to some extent random and made in isolation, or comparatively so. The teacher relies on a bright idea, from whatever source, and the accumulation of bright ideas which constitutes experience. What we need is more linguistic knowledge about the language demands of different situations so that we may plan the balanced, structured schemes of work which we are seeking.

One feature noticeable in several of the topics discussed so far, and arising in particular from our concern with real language in context, is the need for a flow of language in the classroom. Once we have this flow of speech and writing we can work together with the pupils to increase quality and extend range. The flow of language is natural for the vast majority of children, but in the classroom it can only too easily be inhibited by an insistence on standards of accuracy appropriate to a later stage, or on a variety of English 'foreign' to most of the pupils. Without the flow we are left with the study of language in the abstract, of rules which are generally ignored outside the classroom and of words divorced from context. With it our listening, talking, reading and writing stimulate the many language activities dealt with in this book, so that communication, expression, response, exploration, comprehension and so on combine in the pupil's unified language development, which we realize is an essential part of his general development, personal and social as well as intellectual. This is discussed further in the next chapter.

4. Language II

Listening

It sometimes seems that teachers accept as one of the facts of life that children 'do not listen'. Certainly there is a widespread belief that teachers on holiday may be easily recognized because they say everything twice.

The situation in schools is complicated by our need in contemporary society to be selective in our listening, for there is so much noise of so many different kinds that we simply cannot afford to give full attention to all of them. The problem is now appreciated and noise abatement is an important part of anti-pollution campaigns.

In schools, therefore, we must employ the deliberate strategies referred to earlier to ensure that children are trained to listen just as they are guided in the other areas of their language development. If we place due emphasis on listening in the first two or three years in school we shall benefit greatly in all our later language work, provided we do not assume that listening has been 'done' and needs no more attention.

The first step is to make sure that children realize how much importance we attach to listening as a learning activity. In the early years we do not suffer from the complication that appears in the secondary school, where importance is attached to aspects of the curriculum only if they are examined. Until we can change this regrettable attitude, this is a good reason for including listening comprehension tests in our secondary school examinations. The second step is an appreciation of the vital role played by motivation. Any teacher who doubts this should try *whispering* to a busy class (a) 'Turn to page 24 of your Arithmetic book' and (b) 'Would you like a chocolate?', and noting the response. There are more sophisticated ways of demonstrating the need to involve our pupils in the learning process in an active and not just passive way, of course. If the pupils are purely passive the motivation has to be entirely external for many, with all the unfortunate consequences that we know too well.

The *Schools Council Oracy Project* has made an important contribution to our knowledge and understanding of this aspect of language work. In *The quality of listening* [Wilkinson, Stratta and Dudley (1974)] there is a study of poor listening, for example, which comments on our limited attention span as the most important factor and mentions also incidental noise, emotional disturbance and specific blockage as other causes. The project team prepared and published listening-comprehension tests for three age groups, ten-plus, thirteen-plus and seventeen-plus. These may be used as diagnostic tests, as models for internal or external examinations in Britain, as measures of the progress of advanced foreign learners of English or as training material in 'language and education' for teachers or students in training. The authors are well aware of the possible 'danger in training listening and 'listening skills' in isolation'. Indeed, their approach is so much in accord with the main theme of the present work that one paragraph deserves quotation here in full.

> 'As will by now be apparent, the emphasis in our listening tests is rather on the richness and variety of language than upon 'skills'. Significantly, many listening tests and training schemes pay scant attention to the language they use; it is often written language read aloud. Scarcely ever is it considered important enough to quote in reports of investigations. We feel that the motivating force of interesting language, produced not by far-distant literary figures but by people in the world around us, engaged in living and communicating as we do, is a great stimulus to the development of listening ability. We also feel that a knowledge of some of the features of language and how language operates is likely to be useful in this connexion. To put it another way we do not conceive of 'listening skill' as something existing in the abstract, unrelated to such matters as the interest of the material, or the knowledge of the listener—indeed to the whole context.' (*op cit*, page 65)

This is precisely why listening is at the centre of our diagram in Chapter 2.

One final point in this section. We are well aware that pupils should listen to teachers. Many of us appreciate that pupils should listen to each other. We must never forget that teachers, too, should listen.

Talking

There can be no doubt that this is the aspect of English which causes teachers most trouble, in spite of general advances in the last ten years, since the word 'oracy' gained currency. Many of us have deeply ingrained admonitions like 'Silence is golden' and 'Children should be seen and not heard'. Many of us are only too conscious of the time and effort taken to keep classes quiet, and so many who accept the latest thinking on oral work in principle find the practical difficulties daunting. Mostly there is no difficulty in stimulating talk, but the problems of control (of both pupils and talk), of guidance or development and of standards cause many teachers to reply 'Not enough' when asked how much oral work they do. It is the area of least certainty and as such merits a disproportionate amount of space in this survey.

There are three aspects to be considered, the first two of which are not confined to classroom English; they will be dealt with here but referred to again in the chapter on 'Language across the curriculum' (Chapter 6).

(i) Talk as part of the learning process.
(ii) Discussion as a teaching technique.
(iii) Making pupils' talk more effective.

(i) We recognize that some children can pass examinations, and even do well, by repeating the form of words they have learnt by heart, without having a real understanding or grasp of the subject-matter they are handling. Young children need to talk about new knowledge and experiences in order to absorb the ideas involved. Later, some children, usually the more academic, use writing as well as part of this vital process of understanding and assimilation. If we do not encourage children to use language for exploration in this way, we are too easily satisfied with 'penny-in-the-slot' learning, the regurgitation of facts and others' opinions learnt by rote.

One of the most interesting and helpful studies of this process occurs in a discussion document prepared by the project team led by Nancy Martin working on the Schools Council Project on *Writing across the curriculum, eleven-sixteen.* (See *From information to understanding: What children do with new ideas* published by Ward Lock). Two boys, Robert and Terry, had been studying the Upper Thames area and its early inhabitants. Robert's written answer to worksheet questions is quoted and can be seen to be at least adequate and fairly accurate. There then follows a transcript of a conversation between the two boys, started off and occasionally prompted by a member of the project team, in which it becomes clear that their knowledge is inert, that only when they talk does it become used and tested, extended and reshaped. This applies particularly to the central concept of 'porous rock'.

The commentary makes many important points shown clearly in the transcript—explanation and illustration go hand in hand. '. . . . the implications of the information are being drawn, and old knowledge is being brought out and looked at afresh in the light of new.' '. . . . each boy's errors become apparent (to himself and to the other) and are then corrected.' This 'central educational process' demonstrates that, '. . . . The new may be interpreted in the light of the old or the old may be modified to take account of the new'. There is evidence, too, that 'the talking situation seems to produce a motivation that is absent from the written answers'.

The document also shows an appreciation of the practical classroom difficulties. There are just not enough adults to promote and guide the kind of 'learning talk' shown to be so effective and yet time-consuming. Because it is so important, all we can say is that the teacher must plan learning situations which include as much talk of this kind (speculative, exploratory, hypothesizing) as can possibly be managed.

(ii) It is common in the secondary school for pupils to ask if they 'can have a discussion'. They see this as a way of avoiding work, and unfortunately they are often right. The vague, general discussion on such hoary topics as discipline, homework, corporal punishment (which so frequently becomes confused with capital punishment) or pocket money is to be recommended only when there is a live issue to be debated, when homework is excessive, punishment may be unjust or inflation erodes spending power. And then there are other dangers, of course, such as irate headmasters or parents.

The discussion that matters is not contrived or stage-managed in any way. It should occur in almost every lesson because it is an extension of 'talk as part of the learning process'. In some subject areas, such as Mathematics and Science, it will be concerned mainly with methods, approaches and conclusions, because we cannot discuss facts. In others, and especially in English, it is fundamental to all that we do in language and literature.

It is, in short, discussion of the work in hand.

Discussion as a teaching technique is not easy to achieve. It takes patience, perseverance and a willingness to learn by experience, for it depends ultimately on a good relationship with a class. Nor must the teacher deceive himself. It is easy to achieve a great deal of talk in a lesson, only to discover on reflection or analysis that 80%, or at least 50%, of it was contributed by the teacher, leaving between 50% and 20% to be shared amongst 30 pupils (usually in practice amongst half-a-dozen).

It is also worth emphasizing again the point made at the end of the section on listening. The teacher must be prepared to listen, to argue seriously and to accept recommendations for worthwhile reading (for example). Especially in the study of literature, there must be no dictation of response.

(iii) What do we mean by 'making pupils' talk more effective'? There are very many answers to this question, and many attitudes sincerely held by teachers. At one extreme we find those who believe that our aim should be Received Pronunciation used by all our pupils at all times. They are doomed to failure. At the other are those who consider that any interference with a child's speech is harmful and an invasion of privacy. They are opting out as teachers.

So what should we be doing? What standards operate? What does the Bullock Committee mean when it recommends accepting the child's accent?

The first part of the answer takes us back to our earlier discussion (in Chapter 3) of varieties of language. As we grow up we all learn, sometimes the hard way, to adjust our language usage to the total context—we switch codes. In the course of a day, some of us do this many times, all of us do it several times. As with other areas of language usage, some are better than others at it. Our task is to help to appreciate the needs of different situations and to adjust accordingly. In the primary school we shall do this by creating situations with varying demands; in the secondary school we shall usually in addition discuss what is involved—we shall make the knowledge conscious, increasingly as the pupil grows older.

We are not concerned with the beauties of elocution, though we do pay attention to delivery and articulation. We do not seek to eliminate regional accents and dialects, except as they prove a barrier to wider communication, and then our aim is to add a dimension, not to replace. Nor can communication alone be an adequate criterion. We all understand swearing, in intent if not in detail, and every teacher knows what is meant by the pupil who says, 'I ain't done no 'omework'. So we are also teaching the social conventions when we examine appropriate and inappropriate language in various speech situations. We do not, unless we wish to, support the existence of all these conventions, but we do attempt to make our pupils aware of them and then leave to them the decision of flouting them or not.

Our aim may be summarized as twofold:

(a) To enable the child to speak effectively in a wide variety of situations, to switch codes with certainty and ease.
(b) To enable the child to speak clearly and to convey his thoughts adequately. There should in most situations be an equal emphasis on clarity and content.

As with all language work, the teacher must be realistic, stressing, for example, the practical reasons for speaking effectively, including later on interviews for jobs or entry to higher education. Above all the teacher needs to be sensitive and careful in oral work, dealing with consonants before vowels, for instance, because the vowels are much more closely identified with regional and local loyalties. Speech should matter in all English lessons or activities, partly because talk is part of the learning process, partly because discussion is a teaching technique, and partly because ineffective or bad speech should never be ignored. It does not take long or interrupt the flow to tell a boy or girl to speak up, often a basic requirement.

There should occasionally be formal speech activities in the classroom, especially for pupils aged between nine and thirteen, and again when they are older, in the fifth and sixth forms of the secondary school. Suggestions will be found in the sources listed below. Oral examinations, both internal and external, should be encouraged, not least because they give prestige and therefore importance to an aspect of English work sadly neglected until recent years. Speech work should always be part of an activity ('real language in context')—discussion of work in hand, drama, lecturettes, on hobbies and so on. Remember the great value of a good cassette recorder in enabling us to examine speech critically in a way previously impossible; remember also the many fine recordings which we can use in our classroom language activities.

In an attempt to be concise and concentrate on general principles, this section is beginning to sound authoritarian, and this should not happen! The reader is urged to fill in the essential background of theory and classroom practice by reading Wilkinson (1965 both articles), (1971) and (1975); Britton (1967); Wise (1965); Morgan (1966); Skull (1968) and (1969).

Reading

Initial reading is outside the scope of this book, because it is increasingly dealt with in top junior classes and in secondary schools by remedial departments or by withdrawal from ordinary lessons for individual or small group attention. Apart from the useful survey of it in Chapter 7 of the *Bullock report*, one of the most helpful studies of the topic is to be found in *The foundations of language*, Chapters 8, 9 and 10 [Wilkinson, (1971), pages 152–202].

Our concern is rather with the development of reading response, which starts when the mechanical skills have been mastered and continues throughout school life and in many cases into adult reading. It is the theme of Chapter 8 of the *Bullock report*, and of recommendation 94:

> 'Flexible reading strategies, ie the ability to skim, scan, or read intensively as the occasion demands, should be acquired at school and should be exercised throughout the curriculum.' [Bullock (1975) page 524]

This important aspect of English work will be returned to in Chapter 5, because response is seen at its most penetrating and sensitive when dealing with the complexities and subtleties of literature in the later years of the secondary school, and the earlier approach to this appreciation establishes the principles involved.

One relevant point links with the previous consideration of varieties of English. We read many different kinds of writing, from the instructions on a tin of paint to a Shakespearean sonnet. In the classroom, too, our pupils should encounter an appropriately wide range and learn to respond accordingly. The techniques of response, and the development of them, are best seen and understood in the study of literature, even though they apply to many varieties of writing. Once again we are reminded of the *unified* process which is the teaching and learning of English. Very rarely in our response to reading are we concerned solely with the literal meaning; usually questions of tone, intention and emotional content are involved in much of our daily reading.

Because the development of reading skills far beyond the mechanical is so important for later, general progress in school, early detection of and swift attention to backward readers become crucial. Ideally, very few cases of inability to read or poor level of reading should persist into the secondary school. In a less than ideal world, the problem exists at that level. The solution is collaboration with the remedial department and a concerted effort by the English department, an agreed policy which is an important part of the school's total language policy and therefore not confined to the English department, though prompted and guided by it. Such action can follow, as in one known example, from consideration of Bullock recommendation 171:

> 'The English department should consider the development of reading skills at all levels as one of its most important responsibilities.'

Some of the procedures and techniques we need to adopt in order to meet this responsibility are supportive and involve language activities other than pupils' reading. Thus we must encourage them to talk and, increasingly with the able, to write about what they have read, to articulate their response to it. If we dictate or impose a response, however unwittingly, we are damaging development in language and in response to literature. Reading literature is both first- and second-hand experience for the child, and as such is crucial to his development, not least to his emotional progress towards maturity.

Three further points are important in reading development, apart from the considerations which follow in Chapter 5.

1. Pupils should be *read to* frequently and regularly. We recognize this need with very young children, but many of us neglect the practice, certainly in the secondary school and even in the last two years of the primary school. Good reading aloud—and the teacher must ensure that it is prepared and good—has an important part to play in encouraging reading and developing enjoyment and response.

2. Closely linked with listening to stories, sometimes in serial form, is telling stories, either orally or in writing. Here, too, the teacher must take an active part at all stages of development, so that fiction is a shared experience from the infant school to the sixth form.

3. Having demonstrated in these two ways some of the pleasures of fiction, we must ensure that plenty of books are readily available and that the reluctant reader has no excuse that 'it is too much

effort to get a book'. In most primary schools it is comparatively easy to surround the children with shelves or cupboards of attractive books in considerable variety; in most secondary schools it is more difficult, in some perhaps impossible, but careful organization can always solve at least some of the problems.

Writing

So much has been written about writing, it has been explored at so many conferences and workshops, that this section can afford to be highly selective. The many misunderstandings (about 'creative' writing, for instance) have been referred to earlier, and so here we can concentrate on a positive approach.

The guiding principles, as with talking, are the achievement of a flow of written language, of real language in context as far as this is possible in the classroom and, by teacher-pupil discussion, a steady improvement in effectiveness.

We must also cover a variety of types of writing appropriate to the age-group in question. This important topic of categorization has exercised many minds in recent years because of dissatisfaction with the traditional division into narrative, explanation, etc, or the later distinction between personal and impersonal writing. This latter is still of great use, provided that we explore the subject more fully and appreciate the classroom implications of the two types and, moreover, that we realize the categories are not watertight compartments.

There is a very sensible, balanced review of the topic of children's writing in Chapter 6 of *Every English teacher* (Adams and Pearce (1974), pages 75–88). The authors suggest adopting the approach of James Britton rather than that of Michael Halliday (see page 36) because Britton's categories (see note 2 on pages 23–24) arise from the English teaching situation and are more directly useful in planning classroom writing. Transactional writing is 'the language to get things done' and the comments of Anthony Adams and John Pearce are especially helpful in distinguishing the 'service' functions of transactional writing from the social functions. They refer to '. . . the wide range of 'service' functions through which a child's mastery of written language underpins the rest of the curriculum—note-making, record-keeping, recording and giving information, writing history essays and social studies, projects, writing up scientific experiments, and so on' (pages 78–9). Whereas the social functions include '. . . using writing for requests, replies, reports, recording, describing, and handling impressions and ideas' (page 81). Later (page 83) they write:

> 'The lesser formality and the more personal nature of expressive writing make it important in the period when children are beginning to discover and explore their own identities';

and of poetic writing:

> 'The conscious shaping and ordering of experience and feeling may relate to real or imaginary worlds, and must be expected to develop relatively late in the nine to thirteen age range, if at all.'

(Remember that the authors are concentrating on that age range.)

For our immediate purposes we suggest the following conclusions may be drawn. The basic mode of language use, including writing, is the expressive, because it is personal, more immediate and in most cases easier to handle. It should therefore figure in our plans for pupils' writing throughout their school life, including the sixth form. Once the mechanical skills of writing have been mastered, transactional writing should also be covered in steadily increasing proportions, so that by the fourth and fifth secondary years able pupils will be producing equal amounts of transactional and expressive writing in their English work. Poetic writing, the more highly selected, structured and patterned kind, should develop for most after the second year in the secondary school, though this does not preclude earlier introduction of elementary forms of story and verse writing. If we use the cruder division into personal and impersonal, it means that personal writing should predominate in the junior school and well into the secondary school, that impersonal should appear as a small proportion of writing in the third junior year and should then gradually increase its share of attention.

Writing projects, especially in the age-range from nine to fifteen, give an opportunity to develop an integrated, balanced scheme of writing over a period of time, such as a term or half a term. The familiar ones—a novel, chapter by chapter, the desert island sequence, the village series scheme and the broader theme (of exploration, or monsters, for example)—retain their popularity and value while encouraging various types of writing.

Most teachers, however, manage to deal in various ways with the aspects covered so far in this section. The vexed question arising from children's writing is that of accuracy, which generates more heat and false notions than almost any other topic. To be positive, we can say that accuracy (spelling, punctuation, syntax, presentation in general) always matters, but that it does not matter as much as content until we are discussing able pupils in the fifth secondary year. There is thus a sliding scale which it is impossible to define precisely in the abstract, because only the teacher who knows them can decide how much accuracy matters in the writing of a particular ten-year-old group. The teacher has to take into account not only chronological age but also maturity and language development levels. Very rarely could one say that accuracy matters little, and then it would be a case of trying not to inhibit the efforts of a very reluctant writer who managed to produce a few sentences, just as only a stupid teacher would condemn the grammar of a shy boy's very first contribution to group discussion.

It is important, too, to deal with selected errors, especially with less able pupils, in order not to overwhelm and discourage the learners. In the junior school priority should be given to basic sentence patterns, capital letters and full stops; only those who make rapid, sure progress should go on to, for instance, the punctuation of direct speech. At this stage and in the early years of the secondary school, the teacher should pay most attention to common errors (such as confusion-type spelling mistakes) and 'communal' errors (those made by most in a class), bearing in mind the constant need to balance developing accuracy and the encouragement of writing in proper proportions, often a matter of nice judgment. There is more hope of steady progress in accuracy if the teacher does not waste time and effort writing in the correct versions of pupils' mistakes. In this field there is no guarantee of success, but there is more chance of eliminating errors if the teacher simply indicates them and the pupil subsequently identifies and corrects them, with the minimum of help.

Language exercises, spelling and punctuation

The case against language exercises as the framework or structure has been more than adequately made already. There is a place for language exercises when a specific need arises, and especially when communal errors become obvious in a class. But they should be short-term, occupying at most half a lesson, and the need for at least a minimum context should always be borne in mind. Whether or not they should include grammar will be discussed in the next section.

Spelling and punctuation are much more difficult. So far no-one has developed a 100% certain method of teaching them, apart from unacceptable ways which involve physical torture! We have stated earlier that spelling and punctuation (and indeed accuracy in all ways) do matter, that they matter increasingly as the pupil grows older, but they must always be seen against the prime need for a flow of language. It seems clear that, like initial reading, no one approach is likely on its own to be effective in all cases. The individual teacher is recommended to develop his own method of working, using a variety of suggested schemes, by trial and error over a period of time, remembering the points made at the end of the previous section about selection of errors and the need to involve the pupils by stressing the practical reasons for precision. With older pupils who claim, 'I've never been able to spell'—and this proud claim is not unknown amongst postgraduates—motivation is all-important. Unless they are determined to improve their spelling and punctuation, they will make no progress.

Although the best help a teacher can gain is that of group discussion at a school or local level, there are other sources of helpful suggestion. The *Bullock report* contains an interesting Annex A [Bullock (1975), 11.41 to 11.49, pages 181–4] on spelling, which includes a reference to *Success in spelling* [Peters (1970)], another mine of stimulating questions and proposals. Further encouragement and advice are to be found in *Every English teacher* [Adams and Pearce (1974)], in a section headed 'A policy for spelling' (pages 108–110) which includes the claim 'that a policy of saturating children in written-text-brought-to-sound and spoken-language-brought-to-page will be far more productive than reliance on rules or rote-learning of spellings' (though rote-learning has its place in dealing with errors); and in another called simply 'Punctuation' which emphasizes the desirability of stressing the role of punctuation in revealing meaning.

Language study

The writer's views on language study may be examined in some detail in *Language in bilingual communities* [Sharp, (1973)], particularly Chapter 5. It is taken for granted that the more a teacher knows about language the better, but this does not solve the difficult problem of how he gains the desirable knowledge and understanding when he is faced with so many demands on his time and energy. This aspect of the topic, the language education of teachers, will be returned to later under language across the curriculum and in-service training, in Chapters 6 and 9 respectively.

Here our concern is with studying language in the classroom, the deliberate inclusion of explicit knowledge about a language, in this case English, or about language in general. The question is simply whether we include this conscious approach with children. If we think we should, other questions follow, including the proportion of time devoted to studying language at the different ages, and the nature of the study. We must remember always that the criterion for inclusion is contribution to the language development of our pupils.

Traditionally studying language has meant the learning of grammar, to which a great deal of time has been devoted in secondary schools and, even more regrettably, in some primary schools. Doubts have grown about the value of grammar taught in this way, doubts about the validity of Latinate English grammar, about the proportion of pupils who can in fact learn it to any purpose, about the sterility of 'labelling', which so many grammar lessons degenerated into, about the earlier assumption that it was essential for effective writing, and so on. Many teachers were influenced by one or more of these doubts and abandoned grammar as part of the English syllabus, at least on a regular, one-lesson-a-week basis. It would be foolish to suggest that one should avoid grammar like the plague, for many children in the secondary school are learning foreign languages, academic children can learn a great deal of grammar incidentally, and there is no doubt that a knowledge of grammar makes discussion of language easier. What is suggested is that grammar should not occupy a central position, that it should never be taught to those who obviously cannot handle abstractions or analysis, that it should not feature in the primary school and that it should always be justified in terms of its role in the use of and response to real language in context.

Adams and Pearce [(1974), page 10] open up discussion of grammar teaching in this way:

> 'Because many who have succeeded in their educational careers were taught some kind of grammar during those careers, they believe that lessons in clause analysis or the parts of speech were of direct value in helping them to speak or write better English. This is a perfectly natural viewpoint, but it has been put to the test of research on a fairly sophisticated basis and has been found quite without foundation. (For a summary, *see* Andrew Wilkinson's *The foundations of language*, 1971, pages 32–5.)'

Wilkinson's section is headed 'The use of grammar' and in it he briefly reviews developments in grammar during the fifties and sixties, mentioning structural, transformational, and scale and category grammars. He suggests that 'perhaps the best introduction to the grammar of modern English, not tied to any particular theory, is that by Mittins (1962)'. This advice is still valid, especially for teachers. The rest of the section is devoted to a summary of research into the effects of formal grammar, showing, for instance, that training in formal grammar does not improve pupils' composition, that ability in grammar is more related to that in some other subjects than to that in English composition, that a knowledge of grammar is of no general help in correcting faulty usage, that grammar is often taught to children who have not the maturity or intelligence to understand it, and that grammar may hinder the development of children's English by causing confusion. [*See also* Harris (1965)].

Finally he points out that although all the research was carried out with traditional grammar

> '. . . it seems unlikely that the results would prove different with any of the new grammars. They depend on the essential differences between an

analytical categorizing activity and a synthesizing specific activity rather than on the merits of any particular system'.

Since 1971 more new grammars have appeared. Of most note is the long-awaited *A grammar of contemporary English* [Quirk *et al* (1972)], which was followed by a shorter version for university students [Quirk and Greenbaum (1974)] and a workbook. But the position has not changed fundamentally, for no comprehensive treatment of acceptable English grammar which may be adopted directly in schools has yet appeared. Experiments by individuals and groups of teachers will be conducted, as they have been for the past 30 years. The debate continues and changes emphasis from time to time. The last word on grammar has certainly not been said.

Of more obvious value than grammar to all pupils in secondary schools and to older students is the approach to studying language developed in *Language in use* [Doughty, Pearce and Thornton (1971)]. This is a loose-leaf file for teachers which contains 110 units of work, each of which provides suggestions for three, four or more lessons on a specific topic, including patterns of language. The units are arranged in themes under three main headings, but the scheme is flexible and teachers may join units in different combinations, some alternatives being suggested by the authors.

The work meets two fundamental requirements: it is informed by sound linguistic knowledge and it is the result of extensive field work in schools and colleges. These do not make it perfect, but its emphasis is on an appreciation of how language works in society at individual, group and institutional levels and this stress clearly links it with the type of approach recommended throughout the present work. One of our major tasks is to make our pupils aware of language usage, sensitive in their own use and properly critical. The kind of conscious knowledge gained by *Language in use* work is most likely to contribute to language development because it handles language in action and draws on the pupils' total language environment, directing his attention to many aspects of it. Many of the units quite rightly lead the pupil to appreciate the feature under scrutiny by his own observations. The simpler units may be used very occasionally with junior school pupils and more systematically with younger secondary pupils. In the middle and upper forms in the secondary school the work might well occupy a period of time, perhaps two lessons a week for four weeks each term.

Those who do not know *Language in use* are urged to become acquainted with it, and with the companion volume for teachers, *Exploring language* [same authors, (1972)]. Other linked works are published also by Edward Arnold, whose *Explorations in Language Study* series is another source of help and guidance for teachers seeking more knowledge about language. See also the more recent *Teaching English: a linguistic approach* [Keen (1978)].

Further justification of the contribution that language study of this kind, casual and occasional with young children, more systematic with older pupils, can make to progress in the four modes of listening, talking, reading and writing is to be found in Chapter 11, 'Written language' of the *Bullock report*.

The relationship between linguistics and English teaching continues to be explored along various paths. One influential recent book is *Child language, learning and linguistics* [Crystal (1976)]. Professor David Crystal bases his whole case on the need for the teacher (or therapist) to have a firm foundation of systematic knowledge about language (= the principles of modern linguistics), which can be given only by linguistics. He emphasizes the time and hard work required, but at this stage he makes no concrete proposals for initial or in-service training. There are many incidental values in the book, for he does illustrate the attraction of linguistics (if not the hard work!) and he firmly grasps the nettle of conflict between description by the linguist and value-judgment by the teacher.

The heart of the book from our point of view is Chapter 3, 'Language learning'. It starts with a statement of aim:

> 'The role of linguistics . . . . is to inculcate a state of mind, to provide a set of principles which can shape professional attitudes towards specific problems, and which, because they come from a coherent scientific framework, can inspire confidence when it comes to suggesting solutions' (page 60).

The need for a linguistic yardstick is stressed:

> 'It would be very nice if we had available independent measures of complexities of sentence structure—so that we could prove that one sentence was simpler than another, and therefore should be introduced first in any teaching programme' (page 62).

We can accept this without hesitation, but it does underline the long-term nature of Crystal's proposals, both specific and general. What do teachers do in the meantime?

He approves in general terms of the functionalist perspective which he sees as becoming dominant in teaching during the sixties, though he is aware of its limitations, and at the same time he sees the pupil's conscious knowledge as important. He is vague about the nature of this conscious knowledge and the stage at which it should start, but his approach is rigorous throughout. He refers to the linguistic underpinning needed by teachers if they are to benefit from the work of Wilkinson, Britton, Barnes and the *Language in use* team. His solution is a unified approach, an interdisciplinary study leading to agreement on linguistic principles.

Any brief account is bound to be unfair in some respects, if not all. The reader is urged to consult the original. The practical problems remain, however, and Crystal's time-scale is not encouraging. The relationship between linguistics and English teaching is so important that we must maintain our efforts to reach agreement on schemes of language learning for both pupils and teachers. The Language Steering Committee, established jointly by the British Association for Applied Linguistics and the Linguistics Association of Great Britain, is one promising line of development. It includes representatives from the National Association for the Teaching of English and HM Inspectorate, and is at the very beginning of its work, concerned with charting its course. The wider field of relationships between mother-tongue and second or foreign language learning and teaching is being explored by the National Congress on Languages in Education, involving more than 30 professional associations, which started work in 1976.

Summary

At the end of two chapters on language, it seems appropriate to pause in order to abstract the relevant principles so far established to build on the basis of balanced activities suggested in Chapter 2. Some of the principles which follow have been implied rather than explicitly stated. They serve a twofold purpose:
(a) to inform classroom work in English;
(b) to assist in planning (Those of particular relevance to the sub-division of tracks on the diagram on page 20 are marked**.)

      1. The principles remain the same for all ability levels, though pace and the nature of materials will vary according to ability.

** 2. The emphases will change according to the age of the pupils.

      3. The language development of the pupil is always the criterion.

      4. The classroom approach should always be unified—categories are for discussion and planning only.

      5. There should always be a flow of language, oral and written, not discreet items handled separately.

      6. Accuracy should develop slowly and selectively, becoming increasingly important as the pupil grows older.

      7. Whenever possible, various approaches should be combined. (There is rarely one 'right' way.)

      8. The pupil should meet and be required to use as wide a range of English usage as is appropriate to his age and stage of development.

** 9. A list of language functions to be covered by a class should be drawn up.

    10. The teacher's function is 'planned intervention in the child's language development' (*Bullock report*).

**11. Part of the process is keeping records of development.

**12. Unstructured (= informal) oral work has an important role at all stages.

    13. Real language in context is the classroom aim. This means English *appropriate* to the situation, the nature of the occasion and the people involved, not 'one correct English'.

14. Language learning environments should provide a firm base within the pupil's competence and at the same time present a challenge.

15. Our concern is often with the social conventions of language usage as well as the linguistic aspects.

16. Although we make language work as real and properly motivated as possible, we must accept that the classroom is essentially artificial or contrived.

**17. Listening must be seen as important in all language activities. At times it needs special attention and specific development.

18. Talk is part of the learning process; discussion of the work in hand is a teaching technique. Teachers should be aware of these two features at all times.

19. The aim in oral work is:
    (a) to enable the pupil to speak effectively in a wide variety of situations;
    (b) to enable him to speak clearly and to convey his thoughts adequately.

**20. Formal speech activities are most helpful and important between the ages of nine and thirteen, and again in the fifth and sixth forms.

**21. Oral work should always be part of an activity, and not, for instance, repetition of the same item by all pupils in turn.

22. The development of reading response should figure in our classroom plans throughout school life.

23. Reading response must not be limited to literal meaning, but should include also questions of tone, intention and emotional content appropriate to the pupil's level of maturity.

**24. Personal writing should predominate in the junior school and well into the secondary school; impersonal writing should appear in the third junior year and gradually increase in importance.

**25. Writing projects of various types are useful for occasional blocks of work (term or half-term).

26. Accuracy always matters, but not as much as content until the academic forms of the fifth secondary-year.

27. It is important to deal with selected errors, especially common

and communal errors. The teacher should indicate mistakes, the pupil should identify and correct them.

**28. Language exercises should be used only as a short-term measure when a specific need arises.

29. A teacher's personally-developed strategies for spelling and punctuation are most likely to succeed.

**30. In the primary school there should very rarely be any explicit study of language; in the secondary school an awareness of how language works in society is more beneficial than a knowledge of grammar.

5. Literature

Reading development

At the beginning of this chapter it should be again emphasized that English in the classroom is a unitary process, and that the consideration of separate aspects is solely for analysis and discussion. For convenience we may devise a programme which uses the various aspects as labels for periods of time or blocks of work, but there are very few of us foolish enough to attempt a rigid separation of language and literature in the daily work of the classroom—and very many who find the distinction at GCE 'O' level arbitrary and artificial.

The reader is also urged not to see deep significance in the fact that language has been dealt with first and that it has been given two chapters to the one for literature. It is clear by now that language is seen as the basis of the desired approach, but the importance attached to work in literature will become obvious in the course of this chapter, and is reflected in the proportion of time that it is suggested should be devoted to literature. The important recommendation is that literature should not be the only area of language usage to be covered in our English work, while recognizing that in literature language is often at its most subtle, effective and impressive.

In the reading section of Chapter 4 we advocated a wide range of reading materials, of types or varieties of English. In this chapter we are concerned with that band of writing (though it need not be writing) which we call literature, and it would be unprofitable to seek precise definitions, just as it would be out of place here to debate what are the distinguishing features of good and bad literature. We all have working definitions adequate for the kind of overview being undertaken. The fact that we should disagree in detail or when considering particular works is not relevant at the moment. The instructions on a tin of paint are rarely literature (but they may be good or bad as examples of language use); a letter from the Inland Revenue is equally rarely literature, even though it may bring tears to our eyes!

Similarly, limitations of space do not permit justification of the suggestion that we should use in schools a wide range of literature suited to the ability and maturity levels of the pupils, and that not all the works or extracts should be 'great literature'. Naturally we want all reading to be good of its kind, but the essential criterion is the involvement of the reader. We are in a better position to help his reading development if he is reading with enjoyment and response, yet the book is of poor quality, than we are if he rejects or reads only under protest the great poetry or prose we have carefully selected for him. Some teachers defeat their own purpose by suggesting or conveying the impression to their classes that not to read keenly and widely is to be damned, or that to read anything but the very best literature is a sure way to outer darkness.

Of course we want our pupils to acquire the reading habit. Of course we want them to prefer good books and to gain from them all the benefits that we have gained. But we shall not achieve these goals by a frontal assault in the primary and early secondary years, when the key words must be *enjoyment* and *response*. Appreciation in any adult sense or a literary critical approach should not appear until the able forms reach their fourth year in the secondary school, although before then they may have acquired incidentally some of the terminology, for example.

The next three sections, which deal in turn with prose, poetry and drama, are largely concerned with further consideration of reading development. They remain general in their attempt to establish principles to govern practice, while certain specific approaches, such as the thematic, will be dealt with in later chapters. See also *Reading for Meaning: Vol II. The reader's response* (D'Arcy, 1973).

Prose

Nowadays prose literature in schools means novels and short stories. Literary essays, which used to be so popular in secondary school

English syllabuses, have fallen out of favour because they encourage the kind of artificiality which most pupils find difficult to appreciate or to achieve in their own writing and which teachers seek to discourage for the majority. The essay, or a collection of essays, may be studied in the sixth form, and an occasional able third or fourth form may enjoy a limited study of Sir Roger de Coverley, but these are exceptions to the general rule of novels and short stories. The prose anthology also appears, but the handling of extracts varies in scope rather than nature from that of novels. Prose anthologies permit a wider coverage of varying styles in a limited period of time, but for some they can never overcome the essential disadvantage of being a collection of 'snippets'.

These nice distinctions amongst the various forms of prose literature do not concern the primary pupil, or, indeed, many of the less-able secondary pupils. Here we are concerned with stories, which may vary in length but which are otherwise not categorized. In the primary school the problem may unfortunately be different and amount to a serious undervaluation of fiction. The situation has been well described in *Storyhouse: Teacher's book* (Jackson and Pepper (1976), pp v-vi). Once the skill of reading has been mastered,

> '. . . the message the child receives, if he is not a 'backward reader', is twofold. First, the process is now over. He or she has learned to read and this acquired skill must be put to use in gathering together assorted pieces of information for various topics and projects. Secondly, reading stories does not matter as much as other kinds of reading. It becomes a sort of backwater activity confined to the end of the day, when children are too tired to do any 'real' work, or to those otherwise unfilled intervals between the more important activities when they must be kept occupied. In such a classroom it is not surprising that so many children stop reading when they stop learning to read. For children, reading stories is what reading is all about.'

Even if there is no obsession with reading for information, there may be an emphasis on quantity, whereby the child is encouraged to read story after story, and to record 'progress' by tickling titles on a list, without any consideration or formulation of response in the simplest terms. There must be a balance between reading for information and reading stories, and in fiction work part of the teacher's planned intervention must be guidance in the selection of books and stimulation of response, leading progressively from the individual, simple statement in the early reading days to the more complex group or class discussion in the fourth junior year. Even then, we are thinking all the time of enjoyment as the essential ingredient and response in terms far removed from those of literary criticism.

For less able pupils in the secondary school the process should continue in this way, the emphasis remaining on enjoyment and developing response, usually expressed orally. There can be no question of formal study of literature for these pupils, but they can be encouraged to talk about the story (or plot) and the characters (in terms of people they know). For pupils of average or above average ability the approach in the early secondary years is essentially the same—enjoyment and discussion of plot and characters—but there will be a more rapid development of the expression of response, though it may be no more deeply felt. As always, the principles are the same whatever the ability level, but superficial interest is more important for the less able or reluctant, while books for study by academic classes must be capable of standing up to comparatively rigorous examination. With mixed ability groupings, increasingly common in the first two secondary years, there may be some class reading or listening but there is also a need for individual and small group work to cater for varying speeds and degrees of penetration.

This leads us to a further consideration of reading development as it should be encouraged and guided in the secondary school. How should prose work in the classroom be organized? Some teachers abandon class or even group work altogether, and concentrate solely on individual reading, discussion with teacher and occasional writing. This approach ignores one of the most important and helpful aspects of literature, the experience shared amongst a group, in which the joint response enriches the varying individual responses, under the guidance but not dictation of the teacher.

We need to make the best use of different approaches in combination, and we should cater for both intensive and extensive reading, though the time and attention given to each aspect will depend on the ability of the form, as suggested already. In a mixed-ability class we must attempt to provide for all desirable methods.

Intensive reading means the joint study in group or whole class of the same book—in short, the class reader [*see* Calthrop, (1971)]. Much of the reaction against the class reader has been caused by the dreary lessons which have so often resulted from its use—or more properly abuse. To read every word aloud for one lesson a week for a term, or even a year in extreme cases, and to do nothing else with the novel, is teaching nothing of value and is actively discouraging reading for pleasure. Reading aloud round the class—ie choosing readers on any predictable system without giving time for preparation—has further discouraged the reading of fiction and has encouraged 'criminal' activities such as reading ahead, reading preferred matter under cover, and doing Physics homework. The solution to this problem is simple —choose readers and give them time to prepare, or ask the whole class or group to prepare the reading and then choose readers apparently haphazardly but in reality with an eye to their quality and the level of difficulty of the passage.

The solution to the wider problem of the class reader is more sensible organization of the work, including a more concentrated study over, say, half a term, rather than one lesson a week for a longer period. Much of the reading by the pupils should be silent, either for homework or in class if no homework is done. Silent reading should be fostered and trained, because this is the usual adult way. The teacher should choose a number of significant passages from the book, each of which can be covered in a lesson, and these should be read aloud and discussed in turn. The number chosen depends on the number of lessons to be devoted to the book and the number considered desirable for general work on it, but in almost all cases it will include the opening and the conclusion. The aim is twofold:
(a) to achieve as deep an understanding and response as the pupils are capable of;
(b) to relate the passage to the total context of the novel.

(a) involves attention to the basic, literal meaning of the passage, but it must also cover questions of tone, feeling and intention which give literature its impact. As far as possible, the teacher should draw comments and information from the pupils, telling them only as a last resort. In (b) reference back in the novel should always be the task of the pupils, whereas reference forward ('Remember that when we come to the part where . . .') is the teacher's province until some of the class have read far enough ahead.

The last point implies that each pupil has a copy of the book and is encouraged to read it in his own time. It seems iniquitous and self-defeating to involve the pupils in a story and at the end of the lesson to snatch the books away, lock them in a cupboard and promise 'the next thrilling instalment' in a week's time. Reluctant readers are created, not born!

An alternative, valuable approach to the study of the novel is described by Stratta, Dixon and Wilkinson [(1973) pages 67–86]. They pinpoint the two problems of handling a novel in class as length and written language, which many pupils find far from easy. Their solution is 'imaginative re-creation':

> '. . . the re-creation of the experience which the writer wishes to convey is a far more difficult task for the pupil reading a novel than it is for him watching a film or television play, for instance'

and

> '. . . an essential function of novel reading [is] to imaginatively re-create for oneself the experience of the novelist.'

They advocate selection of novels or parts of novels which can be treated in one or more of several ways in order to help the pupil achieve the desired re-creation. The pupil assumes 'a variety of writer roles'. The devices suggested, and described in some detail, are:

(i) The author changes his viewpoint.
(ii) The author as radio writer.
(iii) Re-writing in another context.
(iv) A television or film version.
(v) Translation into drama (single chapters or incidents as plays, rather than the whole novel).

Choice of books for any kind of intensive reading is not easy, as is witnessed by complaints about 'O' level set texts, and is outside the scope of this chapter. In each of the first four years of the secondary school, pupils should study at least two novels in a minimum total of three prose works a year. Prose anthologies and collections of short stories may be included as considered desirable. 'At least two novels' allows for these other forms and also indicates that more than one novel may be dealt with in the same term. Too often teachers seem to adopt a 'standard time' for the class study of a novel, irrespective of its scope and depth. For further advice see 'Suggestions for teachers' in *Begin here: A teacher's resource book* [Way and Dennis (1976)].

The other main responsibility, not accepted as such by some English specialists, is *extensive reading*, the aim being to encourage private reading, to form the reading habit. It takes considerable time and trouble to make good progress in this field. For example, it means that the teacher must get to know children's literature, especially developments in the last fifteen years, and must read many books which he would not read for his own purposes. Indeed, he must accept recommendations from his pupils if he is to be able to discuss books freely and guide selection.

To say that books are needed is to state the obvious. The recommendations for intensive reading involve maintenance of many sets of books, and now we are moving into another area which demands considerable library support. The school library can be used, but its fiction section is usually a blunt instrument for our purpose, even if we can timetable our forms in what is usually at best a private study zone. A system of form libraries has the great advantage that the books in each can be closely controlled by the English teacher to meet the needs and wishes of that particular form. If we have to start from scratch, though, how do we find the books? We squeeze whatever we can from the departmental grant but we rely mainly on donations from the pupils. To ask each member of a form to give a paperback is not much, and in most schools most forms will produce a working library, for the keener pupils will compensate (by giving two or three) for those who cannot or will not provide a book. One word of warning: arrange in advance who is giving what, or you will end up with twenty copies of the same bestseller! The working minimum is obviously one book for each member of the form, but this is equally obviously not a desirable state of affairs. Determination and energy are essential because it is only too easy to bemoan the lack of money for books and make no real effort in this most important aspect of work in English. Our search for suitable books can be aided by recent surveys (eg Whitehead *et al*, 1977) and by the many publications of the School Library Association and the National Book League.

We should operate on the basic principle, admittedly controversial, that we first form the reading habit by encouraging the reading of anything within reason, and then we work to improve the quality of their choice of reading. If we attempt to force the reading of 'good' books, we shall inevitably fail. We work towards improved quality by an increasingly tight control of the books in the form libraries as we progress from first to fifth years, bearing in mind always ability and maturity levels of particular classes. We concentrate on fiction, because other kinds of reading will be stimulated by situational needs or interests, but we interpret fiction as meaning quality of writing, not true or false; so we include, for instance, *The Kon-Tiki expedition* and *King Solomon's ring*. We include some poetry and drama if we think it appropriate for the form, but never if we are working at the minimum level described above.

There are other ways of working towards 'better' books. (Once again we must beg questions of definition.) Occasionally we should discuss books read and ask pupils to give book reviews (and train them to do so less painfully than is usual with first formers). While the form are reading and changing books, we should talk quietly with individuals, eliciting response and suggesting what should be tried next; sometimes we can indicate the superiority of better fiction on the same theme (though not in these terms, of course). We should ask for occasional written work on extensive reading, though not with a weak or hostile form, and with younger children we can use wall charts and other visual records to maintain interest. With all pupils, a record of books read with brief comments, kept at the back of an exercise book, is helpful.

Finally, because it is very easy to develop each of these points at great length, we must emphasize the vital importance of a realistic approach. There is no guarantee of success, and some ways of inviting failure have already been mentioned. Reading fiction is for enjoyment, but it is only one of many pleasant ways of spending leisure time; we must not overstate our case. Similarly, we should never try to make a pupil persist with a book he cannot stand, provided he has made a reasonable effort to become involved in it. We cannot expect reluctant readers to go to any considerable trouble to take books out of a form library; we must therefore operate some simple signing in and out system, run by boys and/or girls, and we must be prepared to accept some loss of books. Accidents do happen, and the only way to preserve a library in perfect condition is to make sure that no-one gets near the books. Whatever we do in this difficult area, we must expect complaints from some parents or head teachers or inspectors about the dearth of the classics in a first form library, or the pernicious influence of the contemporary novels in a fifth or fourth form library. Contemporary fiction causes the most marked reaction, and in my own experience it is just as likely that the complaint will come from a 'progressive' parent who claims that the amount of sex and violence in a form library is well below what it should be if it is to reflect modern fiction truly, as that it will come from a puritan who would like to abolish modern fiction itself. Practical advice is very difficult to give, because circumstances vary so greatly. One does what one thinks is right, arguing the case if necessary, but ultimately one may have to yield to authority—and seek a move if convictions are strong. It is at times like these that one wishes—briefly—that one were dealing with a nice, safe subject like Mathematics.

Poetry

Too often poetry is taught without conviction. This is in part a reflection of society's attitude towards poetry and poets, and in part a result of the teacher's own education in poetry, which in many cases seems to have consisted almost entirely of a limited selection from the Romantics. The teacher's attitude and understanding are even more important in poetry lessons than in dealing with other types of literature, but we must not deceive ourselves into thinking that it is easy to achieve the desired appreciation and feeling, which can then be conveyed with certainty to our pupils.

As with all literature, the keynotes are enjoyment and response. Enjoyment is particularly important here if we are to avoid the indifference and hostility which so often set in during the middle secondary years. Young children enjoy the rhythm of simple poetry such as nursery rhymes—so what do we do to so many of them by their early teens? Yet enjoyment on its own is not enough. We can have superficially successful lessons in which we read poem after poem, agreeing after each one that it was 'interesting' or 'marvellous' or 'jolly good', and doing nothing else. Clearly such work is better than using a poem as the basis for a grammar lesson, but enjoyment rather than tedium or boredom marks limited progress and little, if any, learning.

Our concern, then, must also be with understanding, feeling and the formulation of response in speech or writing if we hope to engage our pupils in listening to or reading poems for pleasure and with a growing appreciation. Remember that we are not thinking in terms of literary criticism until the fourth secondary year with academic forms, and then only at the simplest level. This means, for instance, that we do not deal with the nature and form of the sonnet before this stage, just as we leave technical consideration of the short story till then. Remember, too, that some of our long-cherished beliefs are folk-myths, or at least misunderstandings. To say that children between the ages of ten and thirteen like narrative poems, for example, is not to suggest that these should be their sole poetic diet. To advocate that the teacher should not stand between the pupils and the poem, fussing with immediately irrelevant background information, is not to recommend the negation of the teacher's function (planned intervention).

One could continue in this vein. Perhaps the most important piece of advice for the teacher is that all questions should lead the pupils back to the poem for answers, and not to their atlases or history books, except on those rare occasions when geographical or historical knowledge is essential to understanding (and then, in a poetry lesson, we hope the teacher would tell the pupils). Poems may also be used, of course, for their content or theme as part of a project on a variety of topics. This is valuable because pupils grow accustomed to poetry as part of a wider, more 'normal' concern, but it should never be the only context in which they look at poems. Understanding of and response to poetry must be one of our major considerations in English work.

Of almost equal importance is the fact that there is no such thing as the perfect anthology, because response to poetry is so personal. Teachers should therefore use as many anthologies as money permits and change them round frequently. They should also make their own collections and encourage the pupils to make theirs (individual or group). The reader is advised to seek further inspiration in such books as those by Reeves (1958 and 1965) and Roy Thomas (1961). The principles established there remain valid, while later works have developed new emphases for both teachers and pupils, linking response to poetry with poetry-writing as part of creative work in schools. The importance of this unifying approach cannot be stressed too much.

Many of the relevant points are made in *Explorations* [Jones (1969)], an excellent guide to poetry-writing for children, which has a clear statement as its opening paragraph:

'The purpose of this book is, first, to indicate how the writing of poetry can be a means of bringing children into a deeper understanding of their experience, and of extending this experience (using that word in a very broad sense) in a number of directions; and, second, to indicate that creative writing, and particularly the writing of poetry, is vital not just as a therapeutic device for children with personal difficulties, but for all children.'

The book is well illustrated by children's verse and proceeds step by step. It covers various stimuli, including ballads, sea shanties, clerihews, limericks and advertising jingles. The final chapter emphasizes the value of writing poetry in the sixth form.

The five books of *Touchstones* [Michael and Peter Benton (1968)] demonstrate the close link between poetry appreciation and poetry writing, including the supportive and encouraging use of 'haiku' and 'shape poems' as stimuli. The same authors have developed these ideas and materials further in *Poetry workshop* (1975) for pupils aged thirteen to sixteen. Articles on similar themes may be found in the files of *The use of English* and *English in education*; 'Haiku: the great leveller', for example [Wade (1975)].

It is often good practice to let pupils choose prose *or* verse for their writing. Sound, practical advice like this is given by Jeremy Mulford in 'Writing poetry in the classroom' [in Jones and Mulford (*eds*), (1971)]. For instance, on page 114 we find:

'There may be a case for a teacher banning rhyme on one or two occasions, and there is a strong case for suggesting that children might try writing poetry without it, especially when they have very limited preconceptions about what constitutes poetry. But a ban might well itself amount to an unwarranted imposition. Provided that a child has experienced a wide variety of poetry, both with and without rhyme, it is better to leave him to *decide* in what form he wants to write; for only when he does not feel that he has to work to a prescription will his inner impulse be free to organize what he writes.'

In *Patterns of language* [Stratta, Dixon and Wilkinson (1973), page 44 *et seq*] there is an account of a workshop approach to literature, placing the emphasis on presentation or performance to encourage detailed study of a text. The authors describe work with teachers in several parts of the world to help them explore and grasp this approach, under such headings as poetry and documentary, poetry and collage, and poetry and music. In a similar fashion, *The practice of poetry* [Skelton (1971)], which is both a poet's 'manual' and a guide to the practical criticism and appreciation of verse, is valuable to teachers for the insights it gives. Compare in many respects *Poetry in crosslight* [D M Thomas (1975)]. A last word on poetry writing in schools should go to an article with the intriguing title of 'When in doubt, write a poem' [Protherough (1978)]. In many ways this is a plea for a return to 'a more carefully structured programme of writing activities'.

For a fascinating and helpful brief account of the language aspects of poetry lessons, see 'Language in the classroom', Chapter 14 of

Language and education [Wilkinson (1975)]. The author compares and contrasts simple language analyses of an English language lesson, a science lesson and discussing a poem—eg

> 'The pupils discussing the poem largely determine the direction of the discussion, although the teacher does bring them back to the poem when there is a possibility of the topic being abandoned altogether. Unlike the science lesson, which requires revision of specific material, this lesson allows pupils to initiate their own ideas about the poem, and rely relatively little on direction from the teacher' (page 82).

The implications of such a quotation need to be worked out and discussed, and the practical conclusions need to be tried and modified in the light of classroom experience. But the task is straightforward compared to that faced by the teacher who takes over ('inherits') a third or fourth secondary form hostile to poetry. The ability level is not relevant, for poetry-haters, like reluctant readers, can be found throughout the range. What advice can one give to a teacher in this situation? The comfort is bound to be cold, for many have struggled and some have succeeded, without producing universal solutions, of course, because the point (made earlier in this book) that only the teacher on the spot can appreciate all the factors is specially applicable here. 'Tough verse for tough kids' [*see* Baldwin (1963)] is a line worth trying, though the teacher may be depressed and even suicidal after a series of lessons devoted entirely to poems on such topics as 'Sticky endings' and 'The eight o'clock walk'! More seriously we can say that the key question is, 'Will an attempt to persevere with poetry make matters worse?' There are two ways in which matters can become worse: the hostility to poetry may increase, and the poetry lesson may incite unruly behaviour, even 'riot'. In either case, the only sensible solution is to leave poetry alone for a time, until a growing response in prose or drama lessons suggests that the time is right for another attempt.

Let us hope that the need for such extreme measures will be rare. Poetry is too enjoyable and too important not to figure prominently at all stages of development.

Drama

Drama in schools is such a vast topic that all that can be attempted here is an indication of its value and the place it must occupy. In some secondary schools there is a separate Drama department, which is most effective when it works in close cooperation with the English department, because the major common concern is language development. (For a stimulating discussion of drama and language development, see Bullock (1975), 10.31 to 10.41.) Preferably, some members of the English department should have a special interest and qualifications in drama, so that the greatest possible integration may occur.

The basic problem is that we have to cover both educational drama (or free or spontaneous drama) and scripted drama (or drama as literature and possibly theatre). These are not in watertight compartments, but there are important practical distinctions. Between the ages of eight and thirteen there should be very little scripted drama, the emphasis being on miming and acting out with spontaneous dialogue situations which start with the familiar domestic and community ones and work outwards, especially in the field of imagination. Spontaneous dialogue can be written down, discussed and improved as a next step, though opinions vary as to how soon this should be done. For able pupils and mixed-ability groups scenes from Shakespeare, carefully selected for humour or excitement, can be introduced in the second secondary year and used as a base for tackling a full scripted play in the third year. Other full plays by various authors may be used in the third and fourth years, bearing in mind that it is not necessary to deal in detail with every word or every scene. Unfortunately, there are very few one-act or short plays suitable for use at this level. Those pupils who find the language of Shakespeare, or even of modern authors, a serious obstacle may gain more by continuing with spontaneous drama and creating their own scripts.

Whether or not to develop an interest in theatre is a matter of choice. Without doubt, at all levels drama should be approached in simple terms of production, involving consideration, for example, of how a character would speak, behave, stand, walk or sit, and of the essential layout of the set, because the answers to these questions help the pupils to penetrate and respond to the play. This approach may lead to work in the history of the theatre, for instance, perhaps for a CSE examination in drama, but the criterion of educational value must be strictly applied, because we are also moving into the controversial area of public performance, of 'the school play'. School plays can be most valuable if they are seen as part of the school's work in drama and provided that as many pupils as possible are involved and that all other considerations are not sacrificed to the achievement of a slick, 'professional' presentation. If school plays are merely window-dressing, then they are to be condemned.

Space is essential for classroom drama. A drama studio is desirable but space can be made in even the most unpromising of cluttered classrooms by a determined teacher who cannot gain access to hall or gymnasium. There is always space outside which can be used in good weather. Platforms to provide different levels are highly desirable, as are properties, sound effects and dressing-up boxes. All these may be accumulated slowly over a period of time, often by snapping up unconsidered trifles. These adjuncts are accepted for free drama without hesitation, but the classroom 'acting' of a scripted play is still a controversial matter. Many maintain that to ask older secondary pupils to hold a book, read from it and to interpret the action by gesture and movement, however limited, is to ask the impossible. Others argue equally strongly that in spite of the difficulties and limitations some physical representation of the action is an essential factor in understanding and response.

As in other spheres, there are many possible routes and no one 'correct' way. Like poetry, drama must figure prominently at all levels, but the reader must seek further guidance in specialist works [see Seely (1976); Adland (1964); Alington (1961); Wiles and Garrard (1957); and Slade (1954)]. A few quotations to stimulate thought and discussion seem appropriate here.

(a) '. . . lack of academic ability does not mean that they (adolescents) are necessarily 'gifted' in Art, Handicraft, Metalwork or Woodwork. They usually enjoy these subjects because they are largely non-linguistic; language, whether written, spoken or read is their problem.' [Adland, (1964) page 4]

Does this mean that mime is the best introduction to spontaneous drama?

For those who are 'non-linguistic', should the language always develop from free drama, because the spoken language is usually easier for them? Does it follow that, although such language may eventually be written down, printed (or previously scripted) drama should be avoided?

(b) 'To turn the drama lesson into a reading lesson in which the play is read because it is enjoyable and because 'it makes a change, anyway, from stories', is not wrong or bad teaching in itself. What is so disturbing is the lost opportunity, the failure to seize the play and to wrest some life out of it, to defrost language-frozen minds and so make the printed word and the spoken word a pleasure instead of a problem.' (*ibid*, page 7)

What does it mean if we say that drama should always be treated as drama?

What are your views on reading plays in desks?

(c) 'Much of the shoddy and shapeless work that one sees in children's improvised drama comes from a lack of understanding by their teachers of the true nature of the activity. There is a lot of pointless, and sometimes dangerous, indulgence in emotion for its own sake.' [Seely (1976), page 45].

Consider the kinds of discipline needed in drama lessons of various types with different age-groups.

(d) Excuses for not doing drama:
' "I'd like to do some drama, but . . . .
1. . . . . I'm worried about discipline."
2. . . . . the headmaster complains if there's too much noise."
3. . . . . I don't feel confident to."
4. . . . . I haven't got time."
5. . . . . I don't know where to begin."
6. . . . . once I've begun I don't know how to progress." ' (*ibid*, page 1)

What is *your* excuse?

One further point. There are obvious links between drama and film. Many teachers have found that film appreciation with older pupils (fourth, fifth and sixth forms) has led to faster progress in literary criticism because film makes a more immediate appeal to some. A few teachers have managed to get resources for film making and in this way have covered various aspects of language work, including composition. It is another approach worth considering. Helpful advice and publications may be obtained from the British Film Institute (81, Dean Street, London, W1V 6AA).

Organization of work

Reference has already been made to the traditional secondary school procedure of devoting one lesson a week to prose, one to poetry and one to drama. Blocks of work, concentrated attention to one book, play or collection of poems at a time, have some advantages, the most important being that it is more realistic to read a novel or play for four weeks at three lessons a week rather than for twelve weeks at one lesson a week. These are notional figures, of course, for it is the principle that matters. The details may be decided in various ways to retain the desired flexibility of Chapter 2.

Let us assume five lessons a week and twelve working weeks a term to demonstrate the principle. 'Lessons' as such are not important, for we are really concerned with proportions, so that the scheme can operate in a primary school which has no traditional timetable, but operates an integrated day. Other considerations relevant to integrated studies or humanities projects will be examined in a later chapter.

Remembering that the labelling is solely for organizational convenience, we may devote two lessons a week (= two-fifths of the total English time) to language work, which will always include oral and written composition and other formal oral work, and at the appropriate stages will also cover aspects such as comprehension, summary and language study. This leaves three lessons a week (= three-fifths of the time) for all that we have included in this chapter under the heading of literature.

We may prefer to use these three lessons a week in the traditional way described, but we may decide to consider larger units, for we have 36 lessons a term for literature. There are then two main alternatives:

(a) We follow the diagram in Chapter 2 and work in blocks of a month (= twelve lessons), devoting a month in turn to prose, poetry and drama and giving part of a lesson in each case to the form library (because extensive reading is a continuing process).

(b) We change the scheme in Chapter 2 by drawing six radials instead of nine. We are then working in half-a-term blocks, which can be seen as eighteen lessons or two × nine lessons.

The scheme allows us to vary the length of block according to the scope and depth of the material, and the stage of development of the pupils. The 'persistence factor' is especially important! We may also use the block approach for, eg language study within language work—usually eight lessons in scheme (a) or six or twelve in scheme (b), at two lessons a week in each case. Thematic or project work may occupy all the English time for a term (= 60 lessons)—rarely longer, we hope—or all the so-called literature time (= 36 lessons), or any suitable proportion.

Further discussion might only obscure the principle. Once again it must be emphasized that detailed decisions can properly be made only by those on the spot.

A warning. After spending time and effort devising blocks of work of various kinds for the term and the year, it is tempting to regard them as sacrosanct, to be adhered to, perhaps even with a stopwatch, at all costs. Life in the classroom is not like that, of course, and we must be ready to make minor adjustments to our plans in the course of the term or year. Sometimes more radical interim changes will be needed.

Summary

This list follows and completes that given at the end of Chapter 4 (pages 57–58). Those points of particular relevance to the sub-division of tracks on the diagram in Chapter 2 are again marked**.

31. Literature is for ENJOYMENT.
32. The teacher must also be concerned with the pupil's developing RESPONSE, and the expression of it in speech or writing.
33. The first consideration in the choice of reading is the involve-

ment of the pupils. Any reasonable literature may be used as a starting-point.

34. A literary critical approach is not appropriate before the fourth secondary year, and then only in simplified form with academic streams.

**35. Listening to stories read aloud by the teacher is an important part of the enjoyment of literature at all stages.

36. Plenty of books must be readily available if we are to succeed in encouraging reading.

**37. Reading fiction must never be replaced in the primary school by reading for information. A balanced programme is required.

**38. Shared experience of literature is a valuable part of development. Group or whole class reading and discussion of the same book should be part of our work.

**39. The secondary teacher needs to plan separately for intensive and extensive reading, whereas in the primary school they can be treated as part of one process.

40. Pupils to read aloud should never be chosen on any predictable system.

**41. The organization of classroom literature work in blocks of varying lengths has advantages.

**42. Each year's work in the secondary school should include the study of at least two novels, and a minimum of three prose books altogether.

**43. Form libraries are the best basis for the encouragement of wide reading. Voluntary donation should be sought.

44. We should first form the reading habit by encouraging the reading of anything within reason, and then work to improve the quality of the pupils' choice of reading.

45. Our approach must always be *realistic*. We should set ourselves reasonable targets which may be achieved, and we should always be aware of varying ages, abilities, attitudes and backgrounds in our pupils.

**46. Poetry should be included at all stages. Poetry writing should be encouraged but not forced.

**47. It may be desirable or necessary to abandon poetry lessons for a time if a secondary form is hostile or indifferent.

48. Our concern is with the experience of responding to the poem. To use a poem for information or background in, say, geography or history is valid, but it is not teaching poetry.

**49. Drama work, too, should feature at all stages. Continuity is important.

**50. Free or spontaneous drama with younger children should continue into the secondary school, developing into scripted drama for many and theatre for some.

51. The best approach to drama is in terms of the practical aspects of 'production'.

**52. Dramatic activity should link closely in one of its aspects with language development.

53. Space is essential for drama. Platforms, sound effects and dressing-up materials are desirable.

**54. Film appreciation and film-making should be considered for inclusion with older secondary pupils.

6. Language across the curriculum

Language across the curriculum has come to be accepted as the heading for that area of concern which covers the language needs of all teachers and all aspects of the curriculum, and which therefore raises the question of language study for all teachers. It was used by the Bullock Committee as the title for Chapter 12 of their report.

It centres on English as the medium of teaching and learning, although we must recognize that the various considerations apply equally to all mother tongues. For this reason the area of study is sometimes referred to as language for learning. Whatever its label, we must realize the crucial importance of the mother tongue in the general school progress of all pupils, and we must accept that this kind of language development cannot be restricted to a lesson called 'English'. It is properly the concern of all teachers in all lessons and out-of-class activities. This fact has been more readily appreciated by primary-school teachers, who generally are responsible for the whole or most of the curriculum, in contrast to the traditional secondary school compartmentalism. The point is made in the *Bullock report*, and on page 84 of Schools Council Working Paper 55, *The curriculum in the middle years:*

> 'The secondary school presents a much sharper problem and one which, by all the evidence, has hardly been tackled. Traditional specialist teaching is often based upon practices of learning that take little account of the role of language. Not all teachers recognize the value to a learner of his own linguistic formulations. Writing, for instance, is for many teachers no more than a testing device, a means of retrieving information previously taught. Again, the efforts of many teachers to generate discussion may result in sessions which remain dominated by the teacher and his language. The possibility of moving from an initial tentative formulation in talk to a more reflective formulation in writing is still often unrecognized or ignored.'

Although that paper was published in 1975, it is still true that comparatively little has been done about language across the curriculum, except in certain areas of the country. Certainly our approach lacks coherence and a great deal of misunderstanding prevails in spite of a growing awareness of the problems. Old attitudes persist in many quarters, for instance, so that teachers of science or history or geography may expect the language aspects of their work to be dealt with by the English teacher, and usually they are thinking in very simple terms of spelling and grammar. Some English teachers, on the other hand, may see their task as exclusively aesthetic and concerned solely with the language of literature. The old belief that pupils' utilitarian language can be left to look after itself is no longer valid—if it ever was! But in all this the approach must be unitary, as previously stressed, because for most pupils personal expression in both talk and writing in response to varying demands is the way to achieve command of a range of styles and registers. This emphasizes the need for a cooperative approach within a school, for a language policy agreed by all the teachers.

It is not a simple question of literacy. We all make mistakes, we all have blind spots, though there is no reason to believe, as some would have us believe, that teachers' spelling, punctuation and grammar are getting steadily worse. We are not concerned in this chapter with 'accross' on the blackboard or the child who cannot read the teacher's comment which says, 'Your handwriting is illegible'. We should be concerned about such regrettable lapses, but they are trivial and isolated in most cases when viewed against the vast complexity of language across the curriculum.

An examination of language for learning may well start in a simple way with the consideration of questions asked by the teacher. Sometimes these are non-questions, such as, 'That's right, isn't it?' A teacher may acquire the habit of non-questioning and deceive himself into thinking that he has conducted a searching interrogation. There are closed questions which seek only one answer ('What is the name of the Prime Minister?'), and we should consider carefully when these are appropriate and when inappropriate. There are open questions ('Is he a good Prime Minister?'), which are sometimes replaced in class by apparently open questions, asked by teachers who require a specific verbal formulation and who consistently rephrase pupils' answers. We must ensure that when we ask a class, 'What do you think of that poem?' we do not ignore those who tell us what they think, we really want to know what they think, and we accept *all* reasonable answers.

This kind of critical study of questioning may well lead on to assessment of the language participation of pupils in various types of lesson. What is the proportion of lesson time during which the teacher is talking? What is the total proportion of pupil talk? What is the pupil average?—pupil maximum?—pupil minimum? Is the sequence of talk inevitably teacher—pupil 1—teacher—pupil 2—teacher—pupil 3—teacher—and so on? [For sophisticated exploration *see* Barnes (1976), Barnes and Todd (1977).]

An examination of the social class factors as they affect a particular school may follow. The subject is too vast and complicated for full discussion here, but, in spite of the fact that there is no simple formula by which middle class equals success and working class equals failure, there is a real sense in which some children find the language of the school difficult or even incomprehensible. This may happen in assembly, where the Head always says 'in the vicinity of' and never 'near'; it may happen in the classroom, especially with students or young teachers who have not yet learned to adjust their language to the pupils' level, or with experienced teachers from a different social background who make no attempt to communicate effectively with their pupils. These are simple examples. There is no sharp division of restricted and elaborated codes* between the language of working-class and middle-class children, but progress in school *is* overall more difficult for lower socio-economic groups. Factors other than language are also involved, of course. The work of Professor Basil Bernstein in this field has been so misquoted, misunderstood and misapplied by

---

* These are general linguistic codes which represent ways of organizing meaning. The restricted code has a high level of predictability in its use of language, whereas the elaborated code has a low level, and is in general the kind needed for traditional school learning. The ability to move from one to the other is clearly important. Unfortunately the sociological theory on which these concepts are based was little understood and a crude identification of codes and classes was made by many.

students and teachers that it is only fair to recommend a reading of the work itself. [*See* Bernstein (1971) and (1975)].

This brings us back to the central theme of language and learning, for it emphasizes the difficulties faced by those pupils whose language, for whatever reason, is markedly different from that of the school and inadequate for many classroom purposes. We are conscious of the problems in specific situations, such as that of the immigrant in the Midlands, or that of the Welsh first language pupil who may in an extreme case be said to have 'two second languages'. His Welsh is extremely limited and very different from the Welsh of the school, while his English is sketchy and picked up incidentally in the community. We can recognize that such a Welsh child has no adequate language for learning and is certain to be severely handicapped in his school progress. The language problems of the monoglot English child in the normal classroom are less striking, but they can be just as severe, as we are beginning to appreciate.

Of even wider application, perhaps, is the teacher's need to differentiate between learning the form of words and reproducing it in a test or examination, on the one hand, and real understanding, often gained only by discussion, on the other. One of the best illustrations of this point, based on the concept of 'porous rock', has already been quoted, in Chapter 4 (see pages 41–42).

A similar point was made earlier in this chapter when the quotation from Working Paper 55 included a reference to 'the value to a learner of his own linguistic formulations'. This is why dictated notes are a poor substitute for a pupil's own notes, in spite of protests by teachers that dictation is necessary in order to cover the syllabus and to make sure the pupil 'gets it right'. Dictation often leads to the kind of 'penny-in-the-slot' learning which produces the right words in response to the examination stimulus but which leaves behind no genuine understanding or lasting impression. The *Bullock report* (10.11) suggests that the pupil needs to use language in an exploratory way and that perhaps this can be achieved only in small groups, as opposed to whole classes. It is as well to recognize the difficulty of achieving the full language involvement of the learner, though this is no excuse for abandoning the attempt.

One other main point should be made. In the secondary school the traditional subject areas may raise another language barrier for the less-able pupil. Each subject has its technical language, its register or its jargon, depending on one's attitude. Too often progress in the subject depends on 'learning the language' in this specific sense, and failure may thus be a language failure. Perhaps the best example is the impersonal, passive language of science, known to us all. Why should the young secondary pupil not explore science by personal discovery and personal reporting, even though there are sound reasons why the adult scientist should use traditional modes of expression? In recent years the point has been taken in such approaches as that of Nuffield Science, but overall we do not think enough about some of our ways with language in school, including the language of literary criticism. Should we, for instance, insist upon academic language, a particular form of formal language, for the work of all pupils? If we do, we condemn many pupils to failure and ourselves to frustration and lack of success.

One of the most helpful, recent explorations of technical/non-technical language is that by Professor Andrew Wilkinson in 'Reading across the curriculum' [in Wilkinson and Hammond (*eds*) (1977)]. He outlines the 'language burden':

> 'The notion of 'ordinary language', what Johnson would have called the 'common language of men', is a useful one. We need not define this too closely—it is, for example, the language of conversation, gossip: it is not technical or specialist. The child passing from home to school is required to differentiate his language somewhat. Far greater differentiation is required when he moves from primary to secondary school, for in the secondary school he is introduced in a far greater degree than before to the registers of subjects.'

In the next section he explores the language of subjects by examining seven extracts from different subject exercise books of a fourteen-and-a-half year old girl, before approaching the same area from a different direction by considering the 'complexities in the various reading tasks presented to pupils'. After studying the kind of thinking or quality of understanding required in secondary school subjects, he returns to the fourteen-and-a-half year old girl and states the issues clearly:

'. . . the question of how far the specialist registers are necessary to her learning is raised in acute form. Granted that at some time they are essential, has this time been reached? These questions need to be asked, not by English teachers only, but by the subject specialists themselves, because in the last resort only they have the knowledge to argue and justify. English teachers, however, are not exempt from the exercise. . . . . . .

It is clear why the *Bullock report* emphasized a knowledge of language for all teachers. So often the language becomes what is learnt, instead of the means through which the learning—the concepts, the understandings—are attained.'

Enough has been written to indicate the complex nature and the importance of language across the curriculum. Chapter 12 of the *Bullock report* calls for a school language policy for every school and points to the importance of planning. As elsewhere in the report, emphasis is placed on pupils' talk and its general neglect in secondary schools is regretted. Similarly, attention is drawn to the place of expressive (personal) writing and the fact, already mentioned here, that many pupils need to reach conclusions in a personal use of language. In 12.6 it is suggested that a thirteen year old pupil needed to make 'an expressive statement reflecting his involvement', probably appropriate at that particular stage of development, when he explained how to set up a wormery in these terms:

'I fetched a bucket of soil and a cup. A jar of sand and some chalk. I fetched a wormery glass which you can see through. I made layers of soil then sand and then powdered chalk. I continued like that. Then I put some water in it. I have marked with biro where the water ran. Then I placed four worms in the wormery. They did not stir when they were on top of the soil but later they will. I put the wormery into a dark cupboard which is closed.'

The teacher's judgment as to when and from whom to accept this mode of expression is what language across the curriculum is all about. This in no way denies that all pupils need to master various modes of recording, because they are learning to learn. The teacher's own language is important, too, not least in the essential part it plays in the relationship which encourages the pupil to talk and write, to use and respond to language.

The special position of the English department in the secondary school is another topic for discussion. Members of that department in schools in Britain have a special interest in and responsibility for language (mother-tongue) development. It seems logical that they should provide expert knowledge and advice, perhaps even take the lead in formulating and implementing the school language policy. Circumstances vary, however, and for many reasons the leadership may best come from another department, sometimes because there may be elsewhere a greater knowledge of and involvement in the study of language. With less justification, it has been suggested that the language across the curriculum approach, whereby responsibility for language for learning is spread throughout the staff, is not the best. An alternative would be to establish Language as a distinct curriculum subject and to staff it from the English, Classics and Modern Languages departments, so that the topic would be handled by experts only. This is surely putting the clock back, for the rest of the staff could legitimately claim that language was taken care of by others and that they need not pay attention to it in their lessons. The impetus gained to date for language across the curriculum would thus be lost.

Other chapters of the *Bullock report* raise issues of relevance to language across the curriculum. Topics include the desirability of joint discussions between primary and secondary teachers, even the exchange of assignments (14.13), the importance of the head teacher in establishing and maintaining a language policy (15.31), the role of the advisory service (16.9), the value of special help within the school for probationers (24.3) and the training of teachers as specialist 'language consultants' (24.14).

Many of the recommendations, such as the establishment of local language centres and the provision of long-term courses, depend upon finance and are therefore not likely to be implemented in the near future. Limited and equally valuable local activity is not so dependent on money, however, and much can be done by group work within a large school or in local teachers centres. The questions remain, though. What is a school language policy? How do we formulate, agree and implement such a policy? Where do we start? The *Bullock report* provides many answers, but they need to be unearthed and interpreted in everyday terms.

Advice on where and how to start may be found in *Language across the curriculum: guidelines for schools*, a pamphlet prepared by a group of members of the National Association for the Teaching of English, written by Mike Torbe and published by Ward Lock. It is full of practical suggestions, a fact indicated by the section headings:

What does a language policy involve?

Hints towards starting points.

Who does it?

Possible pitfalls.

What do we do now?

The advice in these sections is supported by 'Some notes on language' and a short reading list. The down-to-earth approach includes checklists for analysing and commenting on recordings of lessons. On page 17 we find:

> 'Amount of time spent on: Teacher monologue
> Teacher/class dialogue
> Teacher/group dialogue
> Teacher/individual pupil dialogue.'

And on the same and the following page:

> '. . . . . A teacher might, when listening to a tape, or watching a video, consider the following:
> the kinds of question he's asking
> how he receives the pupils' contributions
> the number of pupils who contribute, and how often
> the amount of teacher talk
> how often both pupils and teacher misunderstand each other, and why
> lost opportunities, where either pupils or teacher have missed
>   important moments
> use of technical language, and whether it has been understood.'

One other example of the common sense which pervades the pamphlet must suffice:

> 'There are differences between what might happen in a primary or a secondary school, largely because of the size of the staff group. Most primary schools have relatively small staffs, of a size that can work together. But where the staff of a school is too large for everyone to be easily involved, a working group has to be drawn from within the whole staff. Some of the following notes apply to primary and secondary schools equally: others apply only to the one school. Wherever possible, though, it's

best to use existing structures rather than create totally new ones. The familiar group may be the more effective one.

It's also self-evident that, just as with pupils, different members of staff will need different approaches. Some get a lot from working in groups, some from reading books, some from chats or courses, some from visiting speakers. Again, the approaches used, and their successes and failures, can throw light on the whole question of a language and learning policy.'

Further helpful information and advice is available in *Language policies in schools* [Martin *et al* (1977)], *Language for learning* [Wilkinson and Hammond, *(eds)* (1977)] and *Language across the curriculum* [Marland (1977)].

A practical approach, school-based and concentrating on the class-room, is the best hope for developing the language sophistication of all teachers in the short term.

7. Themes, topics and projects; Integrated studies; Team teaching

Chapter 2 adopted traditional ways of dividing the subject 'English' in an attempt to achieve flexible planning of a year's work. Later discussion implicitly assumed such a basis for examining principles and methods involved in such a programme. This chapter looks at radically different ways of organizing English work, usually across the curriculum in the primary school, while in the secondary school the organization may be within the English department or it may be interdisciplinary. No attempt is made here to be exhaustive, but rather the aim is to consider the advantages and disadvantages of approaches alternative to the traditional subject approach.

These alternatives may cover half-a-term's work, a term's work or even the whole programme for a year. Circumstances vary, and much depends on the general school organization and the attitudes of other members of staff, for example, but there is a great deal to be said for a variety of approaches, including the traditional. Thus within English lessons as such, thematic or project work might occupy one or two terms in a year, but not three. In a synthesized scheme, integrated studies or a humanities programme might operate for one, two or three years of a five year course, but preferably not for four or five. It is impossible to be precise about all the possible situations and schemes, so as usual we are thinking of guidelines which may help those on the spot to make decisions.

It is also very difficult in this chapter to be precise in the use of terminology, because there is a great deal of confusion both in published work and in discussion at conferences and courses about the employment of words such as 'theme', 'thematic', 'project', 'integrated studies', 'Humanities schemes' and even 'team teaching'. In one context, Anthony Adams starts a book [Adams (1976)] by writing:

'One difficulty about beginning a book on the Humanities is a prevailing uncertainty about exactly what we mean by the term. It has quickly passed into educational currency: the journals are filled with advertisements that proclaim "an interest in the Humanities will be an advantage".'

He goes on to examine various applications of the word in order to limit the acceptable areas as a basis for discussion. Similarly, Geoffrey Summerfield (1965) writes:

'My use of the term [project] is intended to cover a given range of activities, such as various forms of reading and writing, which are unified by a particular topic or theme . . .'

The rest of his book amplifies and explains this initial position.

There is no need to labour the point. Three areas will be considered—Themes, topics, and projects; Integrated studies; Team teaching—and subtle distinctions within each field will be ignored.

The primary school approach to thematic work and projects is typified by Alan Lynskey's description of his practice:

'I consider a theme to be an area of experience which we share with a class over a period of time, say half a term. The exploration of this area will involve many subjects and activities, amongst them literature, talking, drama, art, writing and music. Through these approaches we aim to involve the child in a rich, integrated area of experience, making it real for him at some point so that personal, creative work can arise.' (Lynskey (1974), page 1).

The essential features are work over an extended period of time on a central theme or topic. Project work in the primary school is most often of the type described by Lynskey, but we can also find the type common in the secondary school, a theme or project entirely within the subject area of English. This may be of a traditional kind, using a literary genre such as parody or a literary theme such as witchcraft, or it may be more widely based yet concentrating on response to literature, as illustrated in *Topics in English* [Summerfield (1965)]. It is worth mentioning here and bearing in mind when we consider the dangers of project work that Summerfield emphasizes what he deems the more important aspect of English teaching, the subjective or personal, though he does not dismiss the objective or factual.

In 1963 appeared *Reflections* (Clements, Dixon and Stratta) which created an interest among English teachers in social themes, such as old age or poverty. As the authors explained again in their later book, *Things being various* (1967) the aim was to cover 'aspects of everyday living experience' likely to engage fourteen–eighteen year olds. Many thematic textbooks appeared as a result of the success of *Reflections*. Among the best of them is the series called *Encounters*, in which John Watts had the same explicit intention: 'The twelve themes which form the framework of this book could be the basis of a social studies course' [page vi of Stage 5, *Point of departure* (1965)]. Experience confirmed that pupils, especially in the fourth and fifth secondary years, were more easily involved in English work of this kind, but the limitations also became apparent. The advice must be that this approach is excellent for, say, a term at a time, but that it should not constitute the complete English programme.

Examples of cooperation with teachers of other subjects in the secondary school, short of complete integrated studies, can be found. These depend on the enthusiasm and initiative of individual teachers or groups, and may be illustrated by a joint English/History project on 'The Elizabethan theatre in its social setting' or a joint English/Art theme of 'Book illustration through the ages'.

Now that we have established in outline the kinds of work we are thinking of, and bearing in mind that many primary school projects contain a greater factual content, perhaps from History or Geography, than Lynskey suggests, we should consider the advantages of themes, topics and projects. Why should we contemplate using them, in one form or another, as part of our English programme?

George Watkins has called projects 'long-term tasks of learning-by-finding-out', probably involving group work (AMA (1973), page 19). This indicates several of the benefits. There is motivation in a definite purpose understood and appreciated by all the class, if the theme is well-chosen to involve them all. There is the possibility in group work of enabling all members of a mixed ability class to work at their own pace and within their capabilities. The approach is flexible and capable of adaptation at all stages. It brings together the various types of skill in English and integrates them in a common purpose. At its best it is a cooperative venture, for the teacher should initiate, stimulate and provide a wealth of material, but should not dominate throughout. Obviously, it allows study in depth over a longer period of time than the usual one or two lessons. It is possible to gain response from pupils to a wide range of literature relevant to the theme. Not only does it involve always the four language skills of listening, talking, reading and writing, but thematic work may cover all or some of the techniques from the media, such as television, film, radio, photography and newspapers. Project work also demands the ability to make notes, including powers of discrimination between major and minor points and the capability of dealing with many types of speech and writing; and the ability to draw together threads from various sources and to co-ordinate and synthesize notes in order to write a report and perhaps reach conclusions. Finally, projects or themes at all stages may well include the need for 'research' and therefore training in the proper use of the library and sources in general.

These benefits in combination seem almost too good to be true, but they may be reaped when themes, topics or projects are working at their best. But they cannot be achieved lightly, by simply saying, 'Let's do a project!' Although the onus is placed on pupils, who become largely responsible for their own work, there is also much hard work for the teacher, first of all in choosing the theme or topic. Then he has the difficult task of knowing what is relevant and available, and of ensuring that it is in the right place at the right time. He must always have more source material then he expects to need. Planning, preparation, organization and consultation (if other teachers are involved) are crucial if the project is to succeed in combining the many, vital aspects of English work listed above. The published 'package deal' project may be attractive and at times of some value, but in general it is essential for a teacher or group of teachers to develop themes and collect relevant material to meet the needs of particular classes and schools. The importance of secretarial and technical support, preferably in a properly equipped resources centre, becomes obvious. It must be acknowledged, therefore, that this kind of work is a severe test of a teacher's ability and control.

Even if the project is properly planned and prepared, there are still dangers to be guarded against. This kind of work may lead, especially in the primary school, to an undue, even exclusive, emphasis on factual writing. It is important that children should be trained in the proper use of reference books and reading for information, but fiction must not be neglected. Whenever possible, project source materials should include both literature and non-fiction, information books. There is little to be said in favour of the primary school which bases all its English work on 'reading for information'. The other danger inherent in fact-finding is well known—merely copying from the source book without any of the digestion, relating, co-ordinating and generally making one's own described earlier. There is no value in stringing together sentences lifted almost at random from a number of information books.

When literature is properly represented among the sources for a project, all may not be well, for literature may become subordinate to the content of the project and not considered for its own sake (see Chapter 5). It may be used purely as a stimulus for some activity other than response to it, and if this is invariably the practice pupils are missing an essential part of English work. There is also a tendency, noticeable in some of the material on social themes developed for use with fourth and fifth forms in the secondary school, to use only short extracts from literature, merely to open discussion on an area of experience, without any consideration of the many other facets which make the total work literature.

If we turn from themes, topics and projects to major schemes of organization known, for example, as Integrated studies or Humanities projects, we find that many of the same advantages and disadvantages occur. In a primary or secondary school, the whole year's work may be planned in this way without any traditional subject divisions and in a manner designed to involve the whole ability range in a sense of purpose all can understand. Alternatively, part of the curriculum may be tackled in this way—perhaps Humanities, or Science, or Environmental studies. Again, this approach may be used throughout the four years of the junior school or the five of the secondary school, or, more usually, for one, two or three years in each case. Various types of integrated studies are examined on pages 33–4 of the aptly named work, *The Humanities jungle* [Adams (1976)], which should be read, anyway, by those who wish to delve more deeply into this area.

Whatever the pattern adopted, the crucial point here is that the guidance of an English specialist is essential. One aspect is stated clearly in the *Bullock report*:

> 'If the child is to meet literature the extent, relevance and quality of that literature must not be a matter of chance but the informed judgment of one who has a wide and detailed knowledge of suitable texts. . . . . it is still too readily assumed that anyone can turn his hand to English. This assumption all too often results in a narrower experience of literature, and the closing of opportunities that might have been opened up had the teacher only known of particular books that match them.' (9.18)

This relates to the point made earlier about the important role of literature in projects, that literature should not be chosen solely for its relevance to the historical, geographical or scientific content of the Integrated studies course.

Of equal importance is the need for English to avoid becoming a mere 'servicing' subject, providing the language medium for the study of other disciplines and not existing as a partner in its own right. Throughout this book we have emphasized the value of the study of a wide range of varieties of English. There is a very real danger that if an English specialist is not consulted, or preferably involved, the types of English used and responded to by the pupils will be determined by the needs of the other subjects included in Integrated studies, and the desirable range will be lost. In contrast we must appreciate that in a properly planned and prepared course involving, say, three or four subjects the pupils' experience of oral and written language will be widened, and literature will not only shed light on other areas but will gain from them to deepen the pupils' experience and response. As with projects, though on a larger scale and involving more teachers, we must not adopt an Integrated studies approach just because it is fashionable. We must justify, plan and prepare if we are to gain the undoubted benefits.

Team teaching, the third topic to be covered briefly in this chapter, can occur in any of the situations already mentioned. It has been suggested that a project covering several subject areas is somewhat of a struggle for a single teacher at any stage of schooling, while team teaching can provide the advantages of mutual support, greater formalization, more planning and the pooling of knowledge and resources. The range of situations suitable for team teaching is almost as wide as the total number of educational situations. At one extreme we have two English teachers (or one English and one History, or one English and one Geography, and so on) whereas at the other we may have in the primary sector the five or six teachers involved in the work of one year of a 500-strong junior school, or the 30 or so teachers responsible for the work of one year in a comprehensive school. The method is infinitely adaptable to both the human and physical resources available and changing circumstances.

Flexibility extends to the detailed organization, so that once again the possibilities are too many and varied for discussion here.

> 'If team teaching is to work, teachers cannot be imprisoned in the straitjacket of prescribed ratios of teachers to children, and in particular the rigid idea of one teacher to one class. Just as some work needs a quiet atmosphere and some can go along happily in a noisy one, so some work can quite properly be taken with large groupings while other work needs small ones.' (Lynskey (1974), page 29).

What other considerations are there, apart from our specialist concern to safeguard the unique contribution of English?

They begin to seem familiar, for they include a clear concept of aims and methods, the ready commitment of the teachers in the team, the monitoring and recording of pupils' progress, the availability of varied accommodation and necessary resources, and the support of others in the total school context (members of staff and parents, for example). Given the necessary platform, the benefits are those to be gained from cooperation, such as the contribution by each teacher of his own expertise, and the greater variety in the lessons and in the pupil/teacher relationships. One advantage that is not so immediately apparent is that in providing a more stimulating learning situation for the pupil we are also placing the teacher in a position to examine his own procedures critically in comparison with those of his colleagues; this may prove painful but it is undoubtedly educational. Two very different books which share a belief in team teaching and an awareness of the problems and provisos are *Team teaching and the teaching of English* [Adams (1971)] and *Teaching from strength* [Worrall *et al* (1970)].

8. Assessment and marking

It is an interesting exercise to look up 'Assessment' in the index of the *Bullock report* and trace the cross-references. We find:

Assessment (*see* also Standards, Diagnosis and Recording)
Standards of English (*see* also Monitoring)
Diagnosis and Diagnostic Teaching (*see* also Screening and Recording)

Under each heading there are many references, providing proof, if we need it, that the field of assessment is a most complicated one. Too often in the past assessment and diagnosis have been considered almost entirely matters of intuition, preferably referred to as professional judgment. Standardized tests, and indeed objective testing of any kind, have been slow to gain acceptance by teachers, though they have been more readily adopted in the primary sector than in the secondary. On the whole, too, schools have not kept sufficiently detailed records of their pupils' attainments and development, and even in some cases where such records have been maintained they have not been used when a pupil has moved from one school to another or from one class to another. We noted in the previous chapter, however, that some approaches involving themes, projects, individual assignments and group work do in fact demand more careful recording than does traditional class teaching.

There has been a tendency for teachers of English, especially secondary school specialists, to distrust national, standardized tests, whether at eleven-plus level or as multiple-choice testing at 'O' or 'A' level of the GCE. The main reason for this is their contention that what can be most easily tested objectively is not the most important part of English proficiency, that an ability to fill in gaps correctly or choose the synonym from a list of four words does not necessarily indicate ability to respond to or write fluent continuous prose. This is why, for example, there were many calls for a composition test to be included in the eleven-plus battery of selection tests.

Concern also focuses on the examining of literature. Experience shows that it is comparatively easy to test knowledge of the content of literature and of what the critics have said, whereas it is extremely difficult to test response to literature, or appreciation. Teachers of English also share the concern of all teachers about the effect that public examinations have on the content and methods of classroom work, again best illustrated by the absence of an eleven-plus composition leading to the abolition of composition writing in some fourth year junior classes. Unlike teachers of linear subjects such as Mathematics and Physics, though, English teachers see no need for frequent testing, which they regard as a waste of valuable teaching time, because language development does not reveal itself in the short term, nor does it occur in a straight line.

Some aspects are outside the scope of this book, except as background factors important for their effect. Types of testing are more varied than they used to be. Apart from the objective and subjective distinction, we need to consider open-book examinations, examinations without time limit, continuous assessment, course work assessment, files of work, Modes 1, 2 and 3 as first introduced at CSE level, and the absence of formal assessment of any kind. It is interesting to note that the original intention that 40% of the school population should not take public examinations has gradually given way to pressure from society for 'a piece of paper' of some kind for all pupils when they leave school. In the public examinations sector we are faced at present with questions about a common examination at sixteen-plus, the replacement of 'A' level by 'N' and 'F', and the introduction of the CEE.

There is also the Assessment of Performance Unit (APU), established by the DES to investigate and make recommendations about the monitoring of standards and the measurement of attainment in general. The progress of the Language Steering Group of the APU, as so far reported, is encouraging, because there is a clear attempt to relate testing in order to determine national standards of performance to language activities which are normally part of the school's curriculum. In *Language performance* (May, 1978—issued by the Department of Education and Science) we read:

> 'We have, therefore, been at pains to propose tasks in reading and writing that take account of some essential features of language, and its use. These include the status of the pupil as the language-user and the situation into which he is put when asked to use language under test conditions. Many of the features of the real-life situation can be simulated by creating a context that demands a purposeful use of language for an identifiable audience. In proposing that pupil performance should be monitored through a response to a wide range of reading and writing tasks, we have sought to emphasize the functional nature of language, which is reflected in the varieties of language met with in the school curriculum. In this way, we hope that the monitoring process will not be something divorced from the learning process, but rather a contribution to it' (page 6).

Monitoring of pupils' performance in reading and writing is scheduled to start this year (1979), with the assessment of oracy, a major problem area, to follow later. The first full results should appear about a year after the initial testing. Other major problems facing the Language Monitoring Team include the width of the ability range to be tested and the comparability over time of marks for writing.

In the context of this book, the range of activities which the team propose to assess is of special interest. For reading these are given on pages 7 and 8, and include reading to gain an overall impression of a single passage or chapter; to select information relevant to a particular topic; to expand upon information previously supplied; to follow a sequence of instructions; to identify the answers to questions by direct reference to a given text; to detect information implied in a passage; to interpret and evaluate a writer's assumptions and intentions and to show an awareness of the characteristics of different kinds of writing; and last but not least, we hope, reading for pleasure.

Of equal relevance to our considerations in Chapter 2, 'Balance of activities', are the lists of writing tasks given on pages 11 and 12 of *Language performance:*

'Tasks for eleven year olds
11.1 Personal response to pictures, music, short quotations from poems or prose, or similar stimuli.

11.2   An autobiographical narrative or anecdote.

11.3   A fictional story.

11.4   A description or account in which the pupil is invited to reflect upon what is described and express his feelings about it.

11.5   An account of something the pupil has learned or read about.

11.6   A verifiable description or account in which the pupil is required to represent faithfully what he has observed.

11.7   An account of how the pupil plans to carry out a task, scheme, or project of some kind.'

Additional tasks for fifteen year olds include, for example, various approaches to the discussion of issues and the solving of problems. At this level, the emphasis is more on 'reflective, analytical writing'.

At present the work of the Language Monitoring Team seems likely to produce benefits for teachers of equal importance to the main work of assessment, even if we allow for the fact that the Steering Group's proposals, put forward for discussion, are bound to change in detail (though probably not in principle) as the work progresses. These almost incidental benefits include the provision of more accurate information about the monitoring of language performance, and an increased awareness of the factors involved in language across the curriculum. The other work of the APU will provide the wider context.

Some secondary schools still have formal internal examinations twice a year, though the majority of those who retain them at all restrict them to once a year. In some schools course work assessment is gradually replacing formal internal examinations and thereby increasing the problem of work-load for the teachers, who are forced to select only a sample of work for assessment. In some schools, several of the methods of assessment mentioned above are used in various and varying combinations.

The wider issues are now receiving a great deal of attention at national level. We can contribute our critical comments when the opportunity is given, but otherwise we can but wait for suggestions, advice, decisions and organization at both national and local levels. Meanwhile it is worth making a number of obvious but sometimes neglected points of special interest and value to the teacher of English.

We cannot stress too much the importance of early diagnosis in, for example, the identification of reading difficulties. Similarly, to continue the same example, continuous diagnosis of reading development is crucial. The *Bullock report* recommends that '. . . the ability to diagnose should be part of the professional competence of every primary school teacher' (17.22) and goes on to state that he needs his own 'observational procedures' and an available range of suitable tests.

A too hasty interpretation of test or examination results may cause injustice. Teachers are sometimes too ready to write off a pupil as 'dim' (a favourite word with some) or lazy without proper investigation. There may be many factors responsible for a poor performance, but the one which concerns us most is the language factor. If we administer tests to a Welsh first language pupil in his second language, English, as used to be the practice, we should not be surprised if he does not do very well, whatever his real ability. Similarly, the language of some standardized tests and examinations is very different from the pupil's own English, a point made more generally about the language of the school. On the other hand, of course, the pupil may be lazy or lack ability, but the important point to remember is that we should find out.

Injustice of another kind may occur. School tests and examinations, both internal and external, must be fair in the sense that they ask questions about knowledge taught or require the exercise of skills trained and practised. They must also be fair in that the candidates should understand exactly what is required of them and should not be faced with the unexpected or trick question. Too many teachers still regard the purpose of an examination as to 'catch out' the pupils, to find out what they do not know. Too many are not prepared to discuss the nature and purposes of the tests they set or to explain the method of assessment. The extreme case, encountered by the writer nearly 30 years ago, is perhaps no longer to be found, but it should serve as a warning. A certain master used to give his third form a test on *Julius Caesar* which consisted of 100 questions, each of which could be answered by one word or a short phrase. Needless to say, they were all factual questions in the sense established earlier. The master was obsessed by the concept of proportion, and the marks he awarded on the *Julius Caesar* test were simply the number of correct answers expressed as a percentage of the number of questions attempted, so that a boy who had 80 correct answers could find that he received the same mark as a boy who had 35. The iniquities of his system were obvious to all but the man himself.

It should be stressed that the previous paragraph refers to what we might call the usual school tests and examinations, which are essentially tests of attainment within a fairly limited range. Diagnostic testing, testing for a particular purpose such as selection, and testing as part of a national survey are examples of practices with different criteria. The prime consideration is the testing and the demands of objectivity and fair sampling across the country may be more important than considerations of the effect on teaching. In many cases the tests are single occasion affairs, with very limited, if any, effect on the school curriculum. Once again, though, the eleven-plus, which led in some cases to the appearance on the timetable of a subject called 'Intelligence', provides the horror story warning of what to avoid. All tests and examinations should ideally encourage the right kind of teaching, in the case of English the range of practice advocated in this book, but at the very least they should never lead to the wrong kind of teaching.

Before looking in detail at marking, we should consider the range of school tests and examinations which is desirable and feasible. There is a long tradition of testing reading and writing in several different ways, and sophistication in language and literature examinations has increased at the same time as newer methods of assessment have been introduced. In a general sense, we know how to measure progress in reading and writing, even though we do not always adopt the best procedures. With listening and talking, in contrast, we are on very much less stable ground. Elocution tests have existed for long enough, but we are only just beginning to develop tests of the kind of oral work we seek to foster in our classrooms (*see* the relevant parts of Chapter 4). The administration of Oral English Tests on any sort of scale is so complex and difficult a task, and the measurement of oral proficiency is so lacking in precision and so subject to social pressures, that many teachers are convinced that we should not test speech in any formal way at all. But there is one very important reason for including a test of oral English in the annual school examination, in public examinations or as part of continuous assessment, unfortunate as the implications of that reason may be.

Any subject or aspect of a subject which is formally assessed achieves status and is regarded as important by both pupils and teachers. This sad fact means that we should examine oral English, even though we cannot do so very efficiently at present. The CSE boards, and some GCE boards, have shown that the administrative problems of oral testing can be solved, though we do not yet know whether all candidates taking an English examination as part of a common examination at sixteen-plus could be coped with. If the determination were there, though, and the necessary finances, ways would be found, as they usually are when it comes to the point. The work of Professor Andrew Wilkinson and his colleagues over the last fifteen years or so has shown how we may improve the validity and reliability of oral tests. If we are convinced, then, as we should be, that oral English assessment matters for both intrinsic and extrinsic reasons, we should press for its inclusion in all public examinations and we should include it in school tests of attainment of whatever type.

Internal school assessment of oral English takes trouble, but it can be organized and is worth doing once a year when the school written examinations are held or when continuous assessment grades are being collected. In schools with a roll of 600 or fewer, it can be done as one operation, but in larger schools it is probably wiser to take it in sections, perhaps by lower, middle or senior sections, or by year groups. It requires the cooperation of the whole staff and considerable organizing ability on the part of the primary head or head of the secondary English department. Half the staff are persuaded to act as examiners, and a briefing meeting is held at which agreement is reached on methods of marking and procedures in general, with taped examples of pupils' talk at varying levels as a basis for discussion. Group discussion by teachers of how to assess other types of English work, using actual examples produced by pupils, is of equal value, incidentally. On the day of the oral tests the school is looked after by half the staff while the other half act as examiners in whatever small rooms and corners can be found. Each pupil may be allowed six minutes, and it is essential that the programme should be adhered to strictly if the whole operation is to be completed, in spite of the temptation to let an interesting candidate go on talking. In six minutes a candidate may give a prepared reading, an unprepared reading and a two minute talk; the prepared reading and six topics for the talk, any one of which he may be asked to speak on, should be issued three weeks in advance; the candidate should be allowed time to look through the 'unprepared' reading passage before reading it aloud. Later, a second meeting of examiners can raise matters of organization and assessment for discussion, in order to improve both aspects on the next occasion. The outline given is a feasible way of testing oral English in a school, though the details may be varied in accordance with preferences or local circumstances.

It seems logical to comment next on that area of assessment in English which has caused difficulty over the years because of its subjectivity, the marking of compositions. Stories of divergences amongst examiners marking the same set of essays and of variations in the marks of the same examiner at different times of day or after a lapse of time were published in the 1930s by Hartog and subsequently by others [Hartog and Rhodes (1935) (1936)]. They led many to believe that the marking of essays was so unreliable that it was not fair to include a test of continuous prose writing in any examination of significance. But the point has already been made that writing of this kind is such a vital part of English work that we cannot ignore it. The alternative is to work to improve the reliability of composition marking, and this was done, first by Wiseman and then by a research team at the University of London Institute of Education for the Schools Council [see Britton, Martin and Rosen (1966)]. The main points to note are that impression marking of English compositions by experienced markers is better than itemized marking which awards so many marks to each category such as content, style, structure and accuracy; that the system of multiple marking used in the Schools Council experiment gave greater reliability and validity than the traditional method; and that the employment of such a marking system by the large-scale GCE boards was practicable. Two further points of definition: 'experienced' means with a minimum of three years' teaching at the relevant level; and the system of multiple marking used involved the addition of three impression marks from three different markers and a separately assessed mark for mechanical accuracy. These are important matters of principle which should be borne in mind by all concerned with public and school examinations, especially in the latter case if promotion or relegation depends on the results. But more everyday matters also demand attention.

Marking is the English teacher's burden. Any legitimate way of lightening the load is to be welcomed, but let us be quite clear that letting the work pile up unmarked in the cupboard is not legitimate. The comments and suggestions which follow apply to the marking of work in English (or any other mother tongue for that matter). They may apply to other subjects, but they do not necessarily do so, because other considerations may arise. See the fuller treatment of English marking in 'Some considerations when marking', Appendix 2 of *Patterns of language* [Stratta, Dixon and Wilkinson (1973)].

1 It is almost entirely a waste of time to correct English work. 'Correct' here means writing in the correct version. It is more economical for the teacher to indicate error, and it is better educationally, too. With academic pupils, the teacher puts a small cross in the margin against a line in which an error occurs. More help is needed by less-able pupils, and for them the cross should be placed by the mistake, or a simple code used (P for punctuation, S for spelling, etc).

The pupils are then trained to find the error and put it right (but not to write it out three times or ten times or 100 times). There is then more chance that they will avoid making the same mistake again, but it cannot be rated more highly than that.

The only time that the correct version should be written in is when a pupil has made a mistake because he has been too ambitious and attempted some use of language beyond the level he has reached.

2 The aim of marking and assessing the normal class and homework is to encourage, and to avoid discouraging. Nothing is more discouraging than a piece of work covered in red ink crosses. With young pupils and with less-able older ones it is necessary to be selective and to concentrate on basics. It is also desirable to select different aspects for attention from week to week.

3 Assessment is the teacher's response to the work as a whole. There are no real objections to giving a numerical or literal grade according to the particular school system, but the most important feature is the comment, which should be on the content, on the interest or lack of it in the story, and should be meaningful as opposed to variations on 'quite good' and 'fair'. Ideally, each piece of work should be discussed with the individual and the comment delivered orally, but in practice this has to be fitted in as often as possible.

It is also encouraging (or deliberately rebuking) to adjust the mark and comment to an individual or to a class, though this must not be done near an external examination for fear of raising false hopes.

4 Decide what you are looking for in assessing compositions. For instance, what balance between content and accuracy is appropriate at different age and ability levels? Be positive in looking for aspects to reward rather than shortcomings to penalize.

5 Quantity is the real problem for the teacher of English. Each class should be doing one major piece of written work each week, as well as several minor pieces. The more conscientious and successful the teacher, the more there is to mark. There are feasible and legitimate ways of reducing the load. Tell the class beforehand what is going to happen, and then mark in detail only a limited amount, such as two pages, a page or half a page according to the kind of writing and the productivity of the class. Similar selectivity is usually necessary with continuous assessment, because the more enthusiastic pupils produce vast folders of work.

The limitation applies to detailed marking only. All that is written must be read by the teacher and commented on.

Do not get into an impossible situation by letting unmarked work pile up. If you are legitimately snowed under, suspend written work until you have caught up, but if this will take more than a week something more fundamental is wrong!

6 It should not be necessary to point out that project work or 'novels' should not be defaced by writing 'Excellent' in red ink across a carefully designed and executed cover. But it is! Comments on this kind of work should always be made on a separate sheet of paper slipped into the folder.

7 Be severe on:
(a) common errors
(b) repeated errors
(c) shoddy work (ie not the best of which the individual is capable).

8 Discuss as frequently as possible—general points with the class or group, specific points with individuals.

Explain what your marks mean and how you decide them. Be prepared to discuss particular assessments and to admit you were wrong if you change your mind on a second reading.

Train pupils to judge for themselves as part of the general development of a critical faculty, including self-criticism. Occasionally read some compositions aloud before collecting them, and let the class make an assessment. Let them suggest a mark or grade but not award it, otherwise the rugger or hockey captain may do very well and the more studious academic rather poorly.

9 It is valuable once a year to mark an age group as a whole, though the unit to be dealt with in this way will vary according to the size and organization of a school. A band would be an obvious unit in a comprehensive school using the banding system.

The marking should be shared by assigning one part of the work of all pupils to each of the English teachers involved. It is also another valuable way of encouraging group consideration and discussion of classroom practice.

10 The final word is one of warning. There is a disease called

'markitis', which may affect all teachers but to which teachers of English seem particularly vulnerable. The major symptom is a belief that one's own marks are divinely inspired and are not open to discussion, still less adjustment. If one awards a composition 14 out of 20, the correct mark is 14 and it could not possibly be 13 or 15; those who think otherwise are at best mistaken and at worst subversive. Teachers marking work in school may take some comfort from the fact that the most acute form of the disease is found in universities, where marks such as B$\pm\pm$ may be bitterly defended.

9. Conclusion

In one sense, no conclusion is possible, for we are in a process of development which has stages but no terminus. But there is value in drawing threads together as best we may in order to establish in summary those principles which should govern our practice. To determine further the context in which our teaching and learning of English occur, we should take note of special problems which are current and which are likely to affect our work during the next ten years, at least. Some points have been made earlier in passing but are included here to complete the picture. Some have not been treated in previous chapters because their impact is not restricted to English teaching, and yet others, of particular concern to teachers of English, deserve a more extended treatment than is possible in this book. In different ways, then, the topics to be mentioned now, and commented on briefly, cannot be ignored when we are drawing up plans of action. The comforting thought is that the principles already established and the approaches suggested provide a way of tackling the problems, even though there are no simple or definitive solutions.

The first problem area is familiar. During the last 30 years or so our educational system has concentrated on organization at the expense of other considerations, including aims. We have developed larger and larger schools, and have broken them down, both vertically and horizontally, into various units. In addition to the original primary/secondary division, we have a range of schools covering middle, junior comprehensive and senior comprehensive, to adopt one set of terms, with variations on each theme until the permutations and combinations seem endless. We may have sixth form colleges or tertiary colleges or split sites. Within the institutions there are very many types of organization to be found, involving perhaps the integrated day or team teaching, year groups or vertical streaming, banding and setting or no streaming at all. The secondary school may be divided into faculties and English become one part of a Humanities department. Something similar may happen in the junior or middle school. The disappearance of English as a subject does not matter—indeed it may be beneficial—provided its peculiar and fundamental concerns are preserved and safeguarded. This means, for example, that literature must be chosen and read for its own sake and that the language used and responded to by the pupils must cover a wide variety.

Whatever the social benefits to be gained from organizational changes on the scale witnessed during the last generation, the effect on teachers and pupils is considerable. There is a danger that organization comes to dominate, absorbing an increasing proportion of the energy and initiative of teachers and perhaps dulling the imagination. Changing circumstances require changing personal relationships and personal relationships within a school are crucial in the teaching of English, though not exclusively so, of course. Some teachers can readily adapt to new and usually larger units, others cannot. All need to appreciate that special efforts are necessary to secure those conditions in which English work can thrive, in which, to take an apparently simply example, pupils are able to write freely and discuss their thoughts and feelings with each other and with the teacher.

In other ways, too, life in school both inside and outside the classroom becomes ever more complicated. In-service training, which used to be spread very thinly, becomes not only desirable but necessary. This is now generally accepted and the argument no longer rages. The machinery is there in the shape of the new, expanded LEA advisory service, but in the present economic climate funding is difficult to find, especially for an improved pupil/teacher ratio to make release for term or half-term courses easier. The most encouraging sign is that in-service provision of all kinds steadily increases, in spite of the very real difficulties.

One aspect of in-service work is of especial interest and concern—language study for teachers. Indeed, the whole question of the proper relationship between linguistics and English teaching is still a live issue, despite the considerable volume of talk and writing on the subject since the mid-1960s. [*See* such works as Doughty and Thornton (1973) and Crystal (1976)]. Although long courses in linguistics are ideal for some teachers or teachers in training, there can be no doubt that for the majority the most productive approach is by discussion of actual classroom 'language happenings', sometimes with the helpful presence of an 'expert', in order to exchange views and work towards the establishing of principles. This is the best hope of achieving the needed increase in sophistication in language work amongst teachers of English. The other relevant point, already covered, extends the consideration to language study for all teachers as a necessary step in the formulation of a language policy for each school as advocated by the *Bullock report*.

Greater sophistication in language teaching and learning would also help us all to counter the argument so often heard that English in schools consists of two distinct if not separate parts. The argument suggests that 'bread and butter' English, basic communication at a simple level, is vital in all learning because in this sense it is the medium of instruction and daily commerce. In contrast, 'aesthetic English' concerned with response to and appreciation of literature is an educational frill and can easily be sacrificed on the utilitarian altar. Such an attitude ignores the many points made in this work about the crucial importance of learning subtle distinctions amongst varieties of English and of responding to literature as part of emotional development. As always, the simple 'logic' of the false argument is widely appealing and convincing, whereas the counter arguments are more difficult to marshal and convey.

This brings us naturally enough to the 'Black Paper' approach. Standards have fallen, the contributors claim, without any evidence. Standards therefore used to be higher, and these higher standards in English were achieved by 'traditional', 'formal' methods, with plenty of grammar, language exercises and learning by heart. The solution to all our problems is thus the simple one of a return to formal methods, with parts of speech, correction of sentences and language drills. But the *Bullock report*, which is in effect an extended answer to the Black Papers, showed that in its surveys very few schools were found to have entirely forsaken formal methods for progressive ways. Other factors must be operating. We can all agree that standards should be higher in order to satisfy the demands of society in the last quarter of the twentieth century, but no-one is able to demonstrate that formal methods are the way to achieve these higher standards. Equally, no-one can produce evidence that the reverse is true, though modern advances in knowledge and experience in schools suggest that the methods advocated in this book are more likely to achieve the desired results.

It is only too easy to find oneself taking up a position at one pole or the other, finding nothing but good in one's own stance and nothing but evil or irresponsibility in the other. A constant theme here has been the need to adopt the best features of all approaches. It would be just as wrong to say that we should never use formal methods as it is to claim that we should always use them. We may believe that formal work on the English language is best restricted to the short term and used to meet a specific need, but that is a far cry from advocating its abolition in the English classrooom. This principle applies in all aspects of English work except where it can be shown that a certain practice is a waste of time or a handicap rather than a help in language development.

Standards were a central concern of the so-called 'Great Debate' on Education in 1977. Much discussion focused on the issue of literacy (and numeracy), which had previously received a great deal of attention and money in the drive for adult literacy. We are faced with a situation in which too many adults cannot read, and clearly we must help them. Our primary task, though, should be to make every effort to ensure that future generations do not suffer the same disadvantage. There is something wrong when we can find secondary schools in which a third of the pupils are in the remedial department, and when students training to be secondary school English specialists consider it necessary to master the techniques of teaching initial reading. It is difficult to extricate ourselves from the present situation, but for both educational and economic reasons we should concentrate our resources on early diagnosis and remedial work long before the secondary school is reached.

Another issue in the Great Debate, the common core curriculum, aroused much less interest. It seemed generally agreed that a common core curriculum already operates in state schools, at least to the extent to which we should wish to see it in force. Disturbing features in some contributions with reference to English were familiar ones, in particular an emphasis on language rather than literature and a stress on content. We can readily agree on broad aims and even on content in a limited sense. What is more important is the choice of attitudes and methods.

Other topics, such as methods of assessment and mixed-ability groupings, have been covered earlier. One extremely difficult problem to which there seems no solution is that of the reluctant reader, a comparatively recent phenomenon, at least on the present scale. Reading is a particular concern of the English teacher, but here we have a problem which seems to be the result of so many causes in the school as a whole and in society as a whole. What happens to the enthusiasm of the vast majority of primary school children? Is this an inevitable process in our kind of society? We need not join the prophets of gloom who suggest that reading will be a lost art by the end of the next generation, for they and their kind have consistently foretold the death of reading since the advent of radio. On the contrary, we must take positive action towards a solution of the reluctant reader problem. The first and most important measure is to make sure as far as is humanly possible that reading is enjoyable for all our pupils and that our literature lessons do not produce leavers who are determined never to read a 'good' book again.

The importance of relationships within the English classroom was mentioned earlier in this chapter. Relationships in a different sense, between departments in a secondary school, also need to be smooth. In recent years, for instance, Drama and English departments have occasionally been at cross purposes, and sometimes at each other's throats. In the primary school there should be no difficulty, for drama should be almost entirely spontaneous or free. We can understand how the problem arises, because during the secondary years most pupils will move at some stage from improvization to scripted drama, and many will go on to study plays as well as 'act' them. The conflict of interest between Drama and English has been greatly exaggerated in some cases, but we must not pretend that there is no problem to tackle. It is part of the wider issue of Drama in Education, because although the English specialist has a professional interest in plays and theatre it may not extend to child drama, and other specialists in the secondary school will also want to use drama as one of their teaching and learning methods. A school staff must face the issues and discuss, for example, the questions posed on page 149 of *Learning through drama* [McGregor, Tate and Robinson (1977)]:

> 'At the curriculum level a number of questions are in urgent need of clarification. What are the specific responsibilities of the drama teacher? What is the related role of teachers of other subjects who want to use drama as part of their general repertoire of teaching techniques? What is the relationship of drama to English teaching? What are the roles of drama in performance in the general cultural life of the school? How can drama best be blended into different kinds of timetables? What are the current patterns of organization? What practical problems exist in this respect and what are the alternative structures? Is there a case for examinations in drama and what issues need to be taken into account in considering this? Finally, what kinds of facilities should be available for the teaching of drama?'

These questions are but a starting point, but they reinforce the need to consider English teaching in its total school and social context.

Another aspect which is of special interest to the teacher of English but which also affects all teachers and pupils is the provision of books. In 1977 a joint statement was issued by the National Association for the Teaching of English and the School Library Association. It expressed concern about the effects of spending restrictions on books and libraries in schools, and suggested that some LEAs were 'choosing the easy way out by quietly effecting cuts in books and materials which are only noticeable to teachers desperately trying to stretch their budgets'. The two associations called on all concerned with education to exercise the utmost vigilance at least to maintain existing standards, and concluded with this sentence:

> 'To reduce the resources available for books in schools strikes directly at the development of literacy and will adversely affect reading for pleasure, leisure and learning.'

Even a short list of special problems affecting the teaching of English now would not be complete without a reference to the difficulties of the multi-racial classroom and school, reflecting those of the multi-racial community. It would be foolhardy to attempt a brief comment, but some idea of the complexities and obstacles can be gained from the fact that it is not unknown for classes to include ten different mother tongues. This raises in its acutest form the question of the medium of teaching, which seems difficult enough in a bilingual country like Wales. Aims and motivation are crucial in determining methods and materials in the teaching of English as a second or foreign language. On one occasion the writer suggested that the aim should be native language proficiency in English by the end of schooling, or earlier. This was accepted without hesitation by the younger members of an immigrant community which made up the audience. Their principal aim was integration with the host community and they rightly saw language as a vital factor. Their elders, in contrast, were more concerned with the preservation of their original culture, dependent on their mother tongue, and believed that low-level communication in English should be the deliberately restrictive aim for their children. Policy and practice are determined by such considerations, and by the estimated length of stay of the immigrant family or community. The various factors are found in different combinations in many places in England, so that there must be constant re-appraisal and change of procedures. Further understanding may be gained by reading *Bilingualism and British education: the dimensions of diversity* (CILT Reports and Papers 14) (1976).

By this stage in the chapter some readers will doubtless be wondering when their own special problems are going to be noted. The intention is not to be exhaustive, however, but rather to draw attention to what are seen as the most complicating factors which affect, and in some cases determine, the teaching and learning of English at the present time. Some of the special problems listed are new, others have been with us for a long time. Some are susceptible to limited, professional solutions, others depend on the attitudes and decisions of society at large. A general reluctance to accept an expert's opinion without discussion is increasingly noticeable as a feature of our contemporary society. Perhaps as a result of this, teachers are much more willing than they used to be to listen to their pupils and students, to consult them rather than dictate to them.

In addition to the special problems common to many if not all schools, there are other particular circumstances which make life difficult in one school or the schools of a certain locality. Thus it may be impossible in one layout of classrooms to conduct a drama or choral reading lesson without serious interference with the work of six other classes. In such a case careful planning and cooperation are essential, as is the determination to resist the temptation of the easy way out—not doing drama or choral reading! As always, awareness is the crucial first step. We may not be able to solve all the problems, but we need to know that they exist and we then hope we can alleviate their effects. A list of problems is sobering but it should not be regarded as depressing, because we can at least work towards solutions.

There are two very real dangers in making piecemeal decisions when planning English work. The first is that if we fail to survey the problems and the advantages in a given situation, we may well run into unforeseen difficulties or we may not use an advantage to best effect. The second is that of making the immediate judgment, or a series of such from week to week, without reference to a unified, global concept of what English in schools is all about. We do not all have the same concept, even in broad outline, nor is it necessary that we should. But it is vital that we should build up and then constantly modify our own concepts in collaboration with other teachers. We need to know, moreover, which methods and activities can happily mix with each other and which are mutually exclusive in that they cancel each other out and merely confuse the pupils.

The view of English taken here covers three aspects:

(a) balance of activities;
(b) methods and approaches;
(c) materials.

Under the first heading an attempt has been made to suggest the kind of structure which many teachers of English seek and which avoids the rigidity of sequencing or the confining effects of too detailed an itemization of the programme of work. Methods and approaches have been the other major concern in this book, while there have been incidental references to materials. Detailed consideration of materials is a separate matter, though.

The kind of survey attempted here is essential. It tries to cover the whole field of English teaching, but it is limited in extent because teachers are busy people and are more likely to read a work of this length. Study in depth of the various aspects is also essential, and the sources for this are suggested in the bibliography. But always to examine the trees may lead to ignorance of the wood. An overall survey is one feature, while the other is a catholic approach which seeks the best practices from many sources, provided they are compatible. In this way a balance amongst the many possible English activities is most likely to be gained, as well as a sense of purpose, direction and ultimately achievement. In all this, though, guiding principles are needed and to express them briefly is an extremely difficult task. The reader may have deduced mine from all that has gone before, but it is likely that different readers will have reached varying conclusions. My most important terms of reference include:

1. English in the classroom should be viewed as a *central part of a liberal education*. This means that we are not solely concerned with the mechanical skills of language, though these are important. Provided these basic skills are not neglected, the development aimed at is ultimately the most useful in the many aspects of life.

2. A balanced programme drawn up as suggested ensures that no part of English work is neglected. Balance does not mean equal attention to all constituent parts, whether these be language skills or types of literature. The flexible structure proposed is the only acceptable kind. The proportions will vary from age group to age group, according to the pupils' ability, and this is a matter for the teacher's professional judgment.

3. The foundation of our work must be the pupil's use of and response to language in a wide variety of contexts. There is no place for work on words in isolation, language exercises or drills except for specific purposes in the short term.

4. Literature is a major area of language usage in which the most subtle use of words may be encountered. Developing response to literature at the appropriate level is a vital part of the pupil's personal, emotional development. The emphasis must be on the stories, novels, poems and plays themselves rather than on background or what is known as 'the hist of Eng lit'.

5. The deciding factor in the choice of literature is the involvement of the pupils. It may be necessary to read literature of relatively poor quality in order to make progress at all, but the need to improve the quality of what is read, talked or written about must be constantly in mind.

6. The combined effect of the first five principles is to emphasize the development of the whole person and not just the intellect. It is comparatively easy in such an approach to English to neglect the intellect and stress too much, for instance, the social aspects of the language. Balance has already been advocated.

7. The determining factor in planning a course is the language development of the pupil.

8. There has been a continual emphasis in this book on the professional judgment of the teacher in the classroom or the group of teachers in the school or locality. An informed decision of this nature depends upon the expert knowledge and advice of all the supporting services in education, including the results of research expressed in classroom terms, channelled through rigorous programmes of initial and in-service training. Often, the profitable approach is the discussion of practical problems in order to establish guiding principles. The cooperation essential to classroom English is not simply that between the pupil and the teacher.

Bibliography

Adams, Anthony (1976) *The Humanities jungle* Ward Lock Educational.

Adams, Anthony (1971) *Team teaching and the teaching of English* Pergamon, Oxford.

Adams, Anthony, and John Pearce (1974) *Every English teacher* (Oxford Studies in Education) Oxford University Press.

Adland, D E (1964) *Group drama: Teacher's book* Longman.

Alington, A F (1961) *Drama and education* Blackwell.

Ashworth, Eric (1973) *Language in the junior school* (Explorations in Language Study) Edward Arnold.

Assistant Masters Association (1973) *The teaching of English in secondary schools* (4th edn) Cambridge University Press.

Baldwin, Michael (1963) *Billy the kid: an anthology of tough verse* Hutchinson Educational.

Barnes, Douglas (1976) *From communication to curriculum* Penguin.

Barnes, Douglas, James Britton and Harold Rosen (1971) *Language, the learner and the school* (rev edn) Penguin.

Barnes, D, and F Todd (1977) *Communication and learning in small groups* Routledge & Kegan Paul.

Benton, Michael, and Peter Benton (1975) *Poetry workshop* The English Universities Press.

Benton, Michael, and Peter Benton (1968) *Touchstones: A teaching anthology, Books 1–5* Hodder & Stoughton.

Bernstein, Basil (1975) *Class, codes and control, Vol 3. Towards a theory of educational transmissions* Routledge & Kegan Paul.

Bernstein, Basil (1971) *Class, codes and control, Vol 1. Theoretical studies towards a sociology of language* Routledge & Kegan Paul.

Britton, James (1970) *Language and learning* Allen Lane The Penguin Press.

Britton, James (*ed*) (1967) *Talking and writing: A handbook for English teachers* Methuen.

Britton, James, *et al* (1975) *The development of writing abilities (eleven–eighteen)* (Schools Council Research Studies) Macmillan.

Britton, James, Nancy Martin and Harold Rosen (1966) *Multiple marking of English compositions* (Schools Council Examinations Bulletin No 12) HMSO.

Bullock, Sir Alan (*Chairman*) (1975) *A language for life (The Bullock report)* HMSO.

Calthrop, Kenyon (1971) *Reading together: An investigation into the use of the class reader* Heinemann for the National Association for the Teaching of English.

CILT (Centre for Information on Language Teaching and Research) (1976) *Bilingualism and British education: the dimensions of diversity* (CILT Reports and Papers 14).

Clements, Simon, John Dixon and Leslie Stratta (1967) *Things being various* Oxford University Press.

Clements, Simon, John Dixon and Leslie Stratta (1963) *Reflections* Oxford University Press.

Cook, Elizabeth (1976) *The ordinary and the fabulous: An introduction to myths, legends and fairy tales* (2nd edn) Cambridge University Press, Cambridge.

Creber, J W P (1972) *Lost for words: Language and educational failure* Penguin.

Creber, J W P (1965) *Sense and sensitivity* University of London Press.

Crystal, David (1976) *Child language, learning and linguistics* Edward Arnold.

D'Arcy, Pat (1973) *Reading for Meaning: Vol 2. The reader's response* Hutchinson for Schools Council.

Dixon, John (1975) *Growth through English set in the perspective of the seventies* Oxford University Press for the National Association for the Teaching of English.

Doughty, Anne, and Peter Doughty *Language and community* (Explorations in Language Study) Edward Arnold.

Doughty, Peter, and Geoffrey Thornton (1973) *Language study, the teacher and the learner* (Explorations in Language Study) Edward Arnold.

Doughty, P S, J J Pearce and G M Thornton (1972) *Exploring language* Edward Arnold.

Doughty, P S, J J Pearce and G M Thornton (1971) *Language in use* Schools Council Programme in Linguistics and English Teaching. Edward Arnold.

Halliday, M A K (1975) *Learning how to mean—Explorations in the development of language* (Explorations in Language Study) Edward Arnold.

Halliday, M A K (1973) *Explorations in the functions of language* (Explorations in Language Study) Edward Arnold.

Halliday, M A K, Angus McIntosh and Peter Strevens (1964) *The linguistic sciences and language teaching* Longman.

Harris, R J (1965) 'The only disturbing feature' *The Use of English*, 16, 3.

Hartog, P J, and E C Rhodes (1936) *The marks of examiners* Macmillan.

Hartog, P J, and E C Rhodes (1935) *An examination of examinations* Macmillan.

Jackson, David, and Dennis Pepper (1976) *Storyhouse: Teacher's book* Oxford University Press.

Jones, Anthony, and Jeremy Mulford (eds) (1971) *Children using language* (Oxford Studies in Education) Oxford University Press.

Jones, Rhodri (1969) *Explorations: a practical study of children writing poetry* McGraw-Hill.

Keen, John (1978) *Teaching English: a linguistic approach* Methuen.

Lynskey, Alan (1974) *Children and themes* (Oxford Studies in Education) Oxford University Press.

Marland, M (1977) *Language across the curriculum* Heinemann Educational.

Marland, M (1975) *The craft of the classroom* Heinemann.

Martin, Nancy *et al* (1977) *Language policies in schools: some aspects and approaches* Ward Lock for Schools Council.

Martin, Nancy *et al* (1976) *Understanding children talking* (Penguin Education) Penguin Books.

Martin, Nancy *et al* (1976) *Writing and learning across the curriculum, eleven-sixteen* Ward Lock for Schools Council.

Mathieson, Margaret (1975) *The preachers of culture: A study of English and its teachers* Unwin Education, Allen & Unwin.

McGregor, Lynn, Maggie Tate and Ken Robinson (1977) *Learning through drama* Heinemann for Schools Council.

Mittins, W H (1962) *A grammar of modern English* Methuen.

Morgan, Diana L (1966) *Living speech in the primary school* Longman.

Muller, H J (1967) *The uses of English* Holt, Rinehart & Winston, New York.

National Association for the Teaching of English (1976) *Language across the curriculum: guidelines for schools* Ward Lock Educational for NATE.

Newsom, John (*Chairman*) (1963) *Half our future (The Newsom report)* HMSO.

Open University (1973) *Educational Studies: A second level course: Language and learning* Open University Press, Bletchley (especially *Block 4: Language in the classroom* and *Block 5: Language and literature*).

Peters, M L (1970) *Success in spelling* University of Cambridge Institute of Education.

Protherough, Robert (1978) 'When in doubt, write a poem' *English in Education* 12, 1, Spring, 1978.

Quirk, R, and S Greenbaum (1974) *A university grammar of English* Longman.

Quirk, R, *et al* (1972) *A grammar of contemporary English* Longman.

Reeves, James (1965) *Understanding poetry* Heinemann.

Reeves, James (1958) *Teaching poetry* Heinemann.

Rosen, Connie, and Harold Rosen (1973) *The language of primary-school children* Penguin Education for the Schools Council, Harmondsworth.

Savage, J F (ed) (1973) *Linguistics for teachers: Selected readings* Science Research Associates, Chicago.

Seely, John (1977) *Dramakit* Oxford University Press.

Seely, John (1976) *In context: Language and drama in the secondary school* (Oxford Studies in Education) Oxford University Press.

Self, D (1975) *Talk: A practical guide to oral work in the secondary school* Ward Lock Educational.

Sharp, Derrick (1973) *Language in bilingual communities* (Explorations in Language Study) Edward Arnold.

Shayer, David (1972) *The teaching of English in schools, 1900–1970* Routledge & Kegan Paul.

Skelton, Robin (1971) *The practice of poetry* Heinemann Educational.

Skull, John (1969) *Speak your mind* Rupert Hart-Davis.

Skull, John (1968) *Spoken English emphasis* Cassell.

Slade, Peter (1954) *Child drama* University of London Press.

Stratta, Leslie, John Dixon and Andrew Wilkinson (1973) *Patterns of language* Heinemann Educational.

Summerfield, Geoffrey (1965) *Topics in English for the secondary school* Batsford.

Thomas, D M (1975) *Poetry in crosslight* Longman.

Thomas, Roy (1961) *How to read a poem* University of London Press.

Thornton, Geoffrey (1974) *Language, experience and school* (Explorations in Language Study) Edward Arnold.

Torbe, M, and R Protherough (eds) (1976) *Classroom encounters: Language and English teaching* Ward Lock Educational in association with the National Association for the Teaching of English.

Tough, Joan (1977) *Talking and learning: A guide to fostering communication skills* Ward Lock Educational for Schools Council.

Tough, Joan (1976) *Listening to children talking: A guide to the appraisal of children's use of language* Ward Lock Educational for Schools Council.

Wade, Barrie (1975) 'Haiku: the great leveller' *English in Education* 9, 2, Summer, 1975.

Wallwork, J F (1978) *Language and people* Heinemann Educational.

Watts, John (1965) *Point of departure—Encounters, Stage 5* Longman.

Way, John, and Keith Dennis (1976) *Begin here: a teacher's resource book* Oxford University Press.

Whitehead, Frank (1970) *Creative experiment: writing and the teacher* Chatto & Windus.

Whitehead, Frank (1966) *The disappearing dais* Chatto & Windus.

Whitehead, Frank, A C Capey, and W Maddren (1975) *Children's reading interests* (Schools Council Working Paper 52) Evans/Methuen Educational.

Whitehead, Frank, et al (1977) *Children and their books* (Schools Council Research Studies) Macmillan Education.

Wiles, J, and A Garrard (1957) *Leap to life!* Chatto & Windus.

Wilkinson, Andrew (1975) *Language and education* (Oxford Studies in Education) Oxford University Press.

Wilkinson, Andrew (1971) *The foundations of language* (Oxford Studies in Education) Oxford University Press.

Wilkinson, Andrew (1965) 'Some aspects of oracy' *NATE Bulletin*, 2, 2.

Wilkinson, Andrew (1965) *Spoken English* (Educational Review. Occasional Publication No 2) University of Birmingham.

Wilkinson, Andrew, and Graham Hammond (*eds*) (1977) *Language for learning* Exeter University School of Education.

Wilkinson, Andrew, Leslie Stratta, and Peter Dudley (1974) *The quality of listening* (Schools Council Research Studies) Macmillan Education.

Wise, Arthur (1965) *Communication in speech* Longman.

Worrall, P *et al* (1970) *Teaching from strength: An introduction to team teaching* Hamish Hamilton.

Acknowledgement

Some of the material in Chapter 2 is reproduced with permission from *English in Wales: A practical guide for teachers* (1977) Schools Council.

Index